RELUCTANT SOLDIER...
PROUD VETERAN

How a cynical Vietnam vet learned to take pride in his service to the USA

Terry L. Nau

(This book is dedicated to my brother Larry, whose love of American History inspired me to complete this project.)

TABLE OF CONTENTS

RELUCTANT SOLDIER ... PROUD VETERAN

PROLOGUE

FORTY YEARS INTO MY NEWSPAPER CAREER, and growing weary of working in the "toy department" night after night, I branched out from my sports editor duties to take on the challenge of publishing a weekly Military Page for the *Pawtucket Times and Woonsocket Call*, two Rhode Island daily publications.

The desire to report on local veterans had been a long time coming for me. I had served in Vietnam in 1967-68, came home to a college campus where one's veteran status was best kept a secret, and buried my feelings for the next three decades.

Finally, while reading a Vietnam book by John Laurence called "The Cat From Hue" in 2002, I went to my computer and searched for the name of my old Army unit, the 2nd Battalion, 32nd Field Artillery, which went by the nickname "Proud Americans." And just like magic, a website devoted to the unit appeared on my computer screen, complete with an email button that led me to the name of an old Army buddy, Bill Kimball.

We had all gone home separately from Vietnam, our leavings spaced out over an entire year. If the Army teaches young soldiers anything, it is the temporary nature of friendships while in uniform. People come into and out of your life with great regularity. A good buddy in basic training disappears, to be replaced by temporary alliances made in advanced training. This shuttle train of friendships culminates with strong bonds of trust formed in a war zone that also end abruptly, to be revived briefly through letters and phone calls before the pull of home sends us scattering to the four corners of the USA.

Soldiers rarely exchanged addresses when they left Vietnam. I only knew that Bill Kimball came from Chicago. This genial section chief rotated back home in the middle of the Tet Offensive. It would be 35 years before we met again, and that reunion became possible through the Internet and the 2/32 website.

At first, my dormant veteran longings began and ended with just seeing some of the soldiers we served with during the war. We accomplished that task with a reunion in Las Vegas in 2003, ironically enough on the same weekend the United States invaded Iraq. But as the years wore on, and my newspaper career waned, the urge to write about veterans became stronger. I approached my editor in January of 2011 about starting a Military Page that would solicit photos from area veterans.

"Sure, go ahead," he said, skeptical of the impact. Within a few weeks, we were getting more photos than we could publish on one page. The Military Page was a big hit. And I began to get inquiries from veterans, or their relatives, telling me about a "good story."

The first one came from the nephew of a World War II veteran from Pawtucket.

"Give my uncle, Anthony Stanis, a call," the nephew said. "He has some good stories to tell."

Anthony was 91 at the time. I was a little skeptical about how coherent he would be. It was a needless worry. Anthony's recall was clear as a bell. And he had some great stories to tell about his days in the infantry, first in Europe and then in the Pacific Theatre, where he witnessed the death of famed war correspondent Ernie Pyle.

GOOD MEMORY – At 91, Anthony Stanis could still clearly recall events from his days as an infantryman in World War II.

"Ernie died because he had a clean uniform on," Stanis recalled.

This all happened on the small island of Ie Shima off the coast of Okinawa on April 18, 1945.

"He shouldn't have been out there with us," Stanis admitted. "Ernie had been on Okinawa for a couple of weeks and he was resting up, just sitting on a ship out in the water. He came ashore for a couple days and spent time with our colonel (Lt. Col. Joseph Coolidge).

"Our colonel decided to take Ernie out to the front. We piled into four Jeeps and off we go. My platoon was supposed to protect him. I had no idea where the colonel was taking us. We came around a corner and all of a sudden, a Japanese machine gun opens up on us. We jumped out of our Jeeps and dove into a ditch. I was 20 yards away from Ernie.

"Major Fyfe, who was our S2 (Intelligence Officer), poked his head out of the ditch after the shooting stopped and asked if everyone was all right. Ernie stood up and said he was okay. A second later, he got hit right in the head by a sniper's bullet.

"A lot of newspaper accounts said it was a machine gun that killed Ernie Pyle but it was actually a sniper. Ernie was dressed in clean fatigues and probably stood out like a neon light," Stanis added. "The rest of us were all in our dirty brown uniforms that blended into the dirt and terrain. It wasn't Ernie's fault. He shouldn't have been out there. It was our colonel's fault that Ernie got killed. I felt pretty bad, too, because we were supposed to be protecting Ernie."

A biography of Ernie Pyle by James Tobin confirmed the details of Anthony Stanis's story. I was immediately struck by the living history that aging World War II veterans were taking with them to the grave. My Military Page could provide an outlet for these stories. And while meeting with a few of these men, I began to uncover my own latent feelings about having served my country, back when Uncle Sam was drafting unformed and nervous teenagers like myself into his war machine.

CHAPTER ONE: DRAFT BAIT

A T THE AGE OF 19, I was either too dumb or too smart to flunk the Selective Service System's intelligence test that determined whether I was mentally qualified to kill people in Vietnam.

"Cassius Clay was too smart to pass that test," my Pennsbury High School pal Jim Mazenko said to me after I somehow qualified to commit military mayhem, even though I went in trying to fail the multiple-choice exam. "And you were too smart to flunk it."

Clay, who revealed his Muslim name of Muhammad Ali to the world after becoming heavyweight boxing champion in February of 1964, had scored a 19 on his draft board exam in Louisville, Ky. and was rated 1-Y, a category that put him on the sidelines until the Vietnam War forced the government to lower its manpower standards in 1966 and draft the controversial athlete.

Me? I went in trying to emulate the Clay/Ali and flunk the test. That seemed like a fast way to avoid the war. But I still managed to get 22 of 100 questions right. That low number would get me into the dreaded infantry with no problem at all. (A passing score was 20!)

"You always were good at multiple-choice tests," Mazenko said, laughing at how my plan to beat the system had failed so pathetically.

Very few members of the "Baby Boomer" generation cared about the military conscription draft until 1966, when a lot of us were 19 years old and moving into the cross-hairs of the draft, which had been around during the Civil War, the first two World Wars and Korea. This was the first American war where young people were beginning to question the government's goal, to stamp out Communism in a country few of us had ever heard about in high school.

More than half of my high school classmates went straight to college and forestalled any draft worries until they graduated four or five years later. A small percentage of the Class of 1965 signed up for the Army. These were the really intense guys who thrived on excitement. Some of their pals opted for the Navy, perhaps believing that might be a good place to ride out a land war.

People like me and Jim Mazenko rolled the dice to see where life would take us. Or maybe we were just standing on the railroad tracks, paralyzed by fear as we waited for the oncoming freight train to run us over. That was probably closer to the truth.

Our good buddy John Coutts, a top-notch athlete, listened to his father and joined the reserves.

"Jimmy (Mazenko) and I were considering our options," Coutts admitted many years later. "My dad came home one day and said 'Why don't you join the Reserves?' That's what I ended up doing. Jim got drafted. Sometimes I wonder what I missed, how my life would have turned out, if I had gone with Jim into the Army." (Jim missed out on Vietnam during his two-year stint in the Army while John went to work in the meat department of a grocery chain, married his wife Joyce and raised three wonderful children.)

If you were 19 years old in 1966, life burst with excitement no matter which road you took. College students went off on their own adventure. They came home from school in the summer of 1966 to see some of their friends stressing over the draft.

"I should quit Penn State and go in the Army with you," my friend Joe Baron said to me one night.

"What are you ... crazy?" I chided Joe. "This isn't an old Hollywood movie where friends join the Army and serve in the same unit. You get sent to Vietnam when your number comes up. We have no control over this. Stay in college, Joe. This war will be over by the time you get out."

We were all victims of the draft in those days ... soldiers, students, working stiffs, protestors, wives, girlfriends, parents. It is hard to explain to young people today how much power local draft boards held over their communities in the mid-1960s. (Politicians finally suspended the draft in 1973 because it was so unfair and unpopular.)

Young people were all in it together in the mid-1960s. This was our generation's war and it wasn't a moral slam-dunk the way World War II had been for our parents.

Looking back over my life, I often think of Vietnam as a world apart, something that happened to a young person whom I barely recognize from the distance of nearly 50 years. Who was the innocent and naïve kid that got drafted and went to war in 1967, afraid that he was never coming back home alive?

A good starting point would be my parents, Daniel and Olive Nau, who came of age during the Depression in Pittsburgh, Pa. My dad dropped out of high school in 10th grade to work in the steel mill and contribute just about all of his earnings to his widowed mother.

"I made seven dollars a week and six of those dollars would go to my mother," Dad would often tell his four sons during one of his "teaching" moments. He started out as a laborer in the Homestead Works in the early 1930s, toiling in the Open Hearth, where steel came pouring out of huge furnaces that reached temperatures of 1,000 degrees during the cooking process.

"We would wear rags on the outside of our boots when we cleaned out the furnaces after they were shut down," Dan Nau told each of his boys when they signed on to work as summer laborers in the steel mill three decades later. "Those rags would catch on fire when we worked in the floor of the furnace, shoveling out hot coals."

Dad missed out on World War II because his job at U.S. Steel placed him in the "essential worker" category. One of his hometown friends, Roddy Clutter, survived the Bataan Death March.

"Roddy was in the wedding party when your mother and I got married in 1940," Dad mentioned to me later on in his life. "Roddy came home from the war but he was never really the same person again."

Dad never completely buried his remorse over staying home to make steel while most men his age served in the military during World War II. His brother Tony fought in the European Theatre and came home with souvenirs taken from German soldiers.

Our family moved 300 miles east, from Pittsburgh to Fairless Hills, Pa., in 1952 as U.S. Steel opened up a new mill on the Delaware River, 20 miles north of Philadelphia. There were promotions involved, and a chance to flee the smoggy air of the Monongahela Valley.

Seems like half of the families who moved into Fairless Hills and neighboring Levittown hailed from Western Pa. And just about all of them came to work in the steel mill.

Our mother also worked, first on the assembly line at Trenton's General Motors plant in the 1950s, and then as a payroll clerk at U.S. Steel for the rest of her working life. Mom's generation laid the basis for women's liberation by going to work during World War II and then returning to work once the children all got into grade school.

The fact that both parents worked was not lost on their children. Each one of the four sons developed strong work ethics in their careers, something passed down from their parents.

There were two rules in the Nau household.

"Number one," Dad would say from time to time, especially after one of us had been caught in some mischief. "You never, ever embarrass your mother."

Number two?

"You're all going to college," said our mother, who finished high school in 1935 and would have gone on to college if she had been born 30 years later. Our parents were like so many other parents we knew. They worked hard to give their children a chance at a better life than the one they had. They knew the value of a college education and stressed it to us at every opportunity.

Mom and Dad produced four boys between 1941 and 1950. Danny came first, then Tim and me and youngest brother Larry. Money was always tight around the house. The boys went to work as soon as they were able. Danny worked in a grocery store meat market when he was 14 ... until he came home and told his parents about the man who lost a finger in the meat slicer that afternoon.

"Oh, I think you're done with that job," Mom told him.

Tim and Larry and I got into the newspaper business, delivering the morning paper before school or the afternoon paper after school. You could make two or three dollars a week delivering papers, money we sometimes saved for big gifts, like the rabbit-hunting hound dog Tim and I bought for $35 in 1960.

FADED PHOTOGRAPH – Dan Nau Sr. poses with his sons Dan Jr., Terry, Larry and Tim in 1967 when three of the boys were serving in the U.S. Armed Forces. (Photo by Olive Nau)

Our father taught us how to handle shotguns before we became old enough to hunt small game (rabbits and pheasants) when we turned 12. Bucks County still had plenty of farm country in the 1950s. Hunting and fishing were a way of life for many residents.

On Saturday mornings in the fall, Dad would pile at least two of his boys into the car along with his prized English setter "Dinah" and off we would go, hunting four hours in the morning, breaking for lunch, and then traversing the corn fields until the sun went down.

Dinah would fall asleep leaning against Dad on the car ride home. We would "gut" the game we killed in the field, then bring the bloody carcasses home to our ever-tolerant mother, who would complete the cleaning process and then serve us pheasant and rabbit for the next week.

Dad was a big sports fan who loved baseball above all else. He would often play catch with one or two of his sons in the front yard, telling us stories of his too-short high school career in between throws. He also took great pleasure in listening to his beloved Pittsburgh Pirates on a transistor radio. One night in 1959, Dad's radio penetrated through the plywood-thin walls of our home, relaying the news of Harvey Haddix's perfect pitching for the Pirates. Dad was listening in his bedroom until he couldn't stand being alone.

"Boys," he said, barging into our room. "Haddix has a perfect game in the ninth inning!" And then he sat there on the edge of the bed Tim and I shared, until the Milwaukee Braves broke through in the 13th inning. The Pirates somehow lost that game but they would defeat the hated New York Yankees to win the World Series in 1960, much to the delight of all the transplanted Western Pa. natives now living in the southeastern corner of the state, in Phillies country.

In January of 1961, Dad came home from work early in the evening, five hours before his shift was supposed to end. He looked pale as he retired to his bedroom. Mom was working her shift at General Motors until midnight.

Around 11 o'clock, Dad came into our room in his pajamas, and slowly sat down on our bed, gathering his three youngest boys around him. He talked to each of us, told us how much he loved us, and then said "good-bye." He was trying to "walk through" the pain of a massive heart attack and didn't think he would make it through the night. That's how men handled things in his mind.

Dan Nau did survive the night. An electrocardiogram the next morning confirmed a massive heart attack. The muscle in Dad's heart was severely damaged. Our tower of strength spent the next two years recovering. He would refrain from hunting and many other strenuous activities over the final eight years of his life. He died almost instantly from his second heart attack at the age of 53 on March 9, 1969 while driving out of the steel mill following a Saturday night shift.

We always felt like the steel mill killed him, which is why there was a third family rule added to the list: None of the boys would make a career of working for United States Steel.

The 1960s are usually portrayed as a time of great turmoil, wonderful music, protestors singing anti-war tunes in the street, Civil Rights marches, shocking murders of three national political leaders … the list goes on and on. I endured my own turmoil, getting drafted in 1966 at the age of 19 years and three months and taking a slow train down to Fort Jackson, S.C. to begin what I later learned to appreciate as the most exciting and formative two years of my life.

Back in the mid-1960s, every young man feared the Selective Service draft machine, which weighed heavily over the lives of males between the ages of 18 and 26. As the Vietnam "conflict" heated up, the Selective Service stoked its conscription machine, dropping the age for induction from 21 to 19 as 1965 turned into 1966.

Some of the more creative souls worked the outer edges of the military conscription system. At a pre-induction physical examination, I met a kid who stepped on the scales and hit the 105-pound marker. He was declared underweight and sent home.

"Had to quit eating for two months," he said to a group of us while putting his clothes back on. "Ain't no way I'm going to Vietnam!"

I was pretty naive about the draft process. The law stated you had to sign up within one month of your 18th birthday. My family and I were on vacation in the Pocono Mountains when I turned 18 in late June of 1965. Returning home a week later, I went to work on a local golf course, finally heading to the draft board in nearby Bristol 17 days after my birthday. Still plenty of time, I thought, to sign up for the draft.

"Where have you been, young man?" the lady behind the counter asked me. She pressed a button on her phone and soon a white-haired man appeared in front of me.

"You're not a draft dodger are you, son?" he inquired, sizing me up from top to bottom.

"No, sir. I was on vacation," I offered.

"For three weeks?"

"I didn't know I was late yet. The law says I have a month to sign up."

"A diligent youngster would sign up for the draft as soon as possible, especially during a time of war," the old man said. They made me fill out a form and sent me home. I didn't realize it at the time but the white-haired fellow was a World War I veteran and head of the local draft board. The alleged Gulf of Tonkin incident in 1964 that triggered President Johnson's decision to step up pressure on Vietnam had raised the stakes for draft board officials. They were all under pressure to meet manpower demands as LBJ expanded a minor conflict into a full-scale war.

The beating drums of the anti-war movement could be heard in the distance, even though it was just 1965 and Johnson had been elected by a landslide the year before. Anyone could be a draft-dodger, at least in a World War I veteran's eyes. People were already burning their draft cards at protest rallies. Scenes of anti-war protestors torching their draft cards were shown on national television and treated with some disdain by the commentators.

In August of 1965, Congress enacted a law to broaden draft card violations and punish anyone who "knowingly destroys or mutilates" his ticket into the army. The stakes were getting higher.

After Dad's heart attack, his four boys did what they could to help out around the house. Oldest son Dan came home from college and worked in the steel mill to support the family, turning over his paycheck to his mother, the same way his father did in the 1930s.

Tim graduated high school in 1963, then joined the Air Force for four years so his parents didn't have to take on the expense of putting him through college.

Dad came home from the airport after sending his second son off to basic training in Texas, sat down and put his head in his hands, uncertain as to why Tim had chosen the Air Force over college. Our parents' plan for sending four sons through college seemed to be falling apart. Danny dropped out of school for nearly two years. Tim joined the Air Force. Larry and I were hardly stellar students.

If the 1950s had been a decade of simple living under President Eisenhower, the 1960s were becoming a bit more complicated, both for our family and the nation. New President John Fitzgerald Kennedy made a big mistake early in his first term, signing off on the CIA's planned invasion of Cuba that quickly went awry. In October of 1962, he found himself staring down Soviet Premier Nikita Khrushchev in a nuclear missile crisis after the Russians began installing missile silos in Cuba, just 90 miles from Florida.

Families gathered around their television sets during that 13-day showdown, wondering if the world was coming to an end. It wasn't such a crazy notion. In the 1950s, Americans had been encouraged to build nuclear bomb shelters in our backyards. Kids were taught to hide under desks at school during fire drills, as though that might save them from nuclear obliteration.

Kennedy continued the use of military "advisers" in South Vietnam, sustaining a policy begun by Eisenhower after the French got thrown out of Vietnam in 1954. Ike, who knew something about war, avoided sending combat soldiers to Vietnam. Kennedy upped our troop levels in Vietnam from 3,000 in 1961 to 16,300 advisers in 1963. Some of his defenders say JFK planned to pull us out of Vietnam during his second term in office, had he lived to see the day.

Vietnam was not a word we heard very often in the news, or at school. My American History teacher debated his 10th grade class one day in 1963 about an obscure slogan that dated back nearly 100 years – "My country, right or wrong." Patriotic citizens took those words to mean the United States could do no wrong. It had fought to free the slaves in the Civil War, backed Europe against the Germans in two world wars, and even risked its young soldiers in far-away Korea in 1950. The USA was always right, or so our young minds thought.

"It's not just my country right or wrong," the teacher warned us. "It's our duty as citizens to follow our country when it is right, and our duty to disagree with our leaders when we think they are wrong."

Few of us considered the latter option in 1963. We were stunned in November when JFK was murdered in the streets of Dallas by an assassin with ties to the Soviet Union. Vice President Lyndon Johnson assumed the Presidency as the nation mourned. LBJ vowed to continue Kennedy's policies, including the one in Vietnam. Hardly any of us noticed. Vietnam seemed like a phonograph record playing in the background. We could hardly hear the music.

I graduated high school in 1965 and went to work in the steel mill, thinking I could save enough money in one year to pay for college. The steel mill paid pretty good money in those days for a young kid out of high school with no skills – $3.25 per hour and if you were lucky, the bosses would let you work 16 hours in a row, the second eight at time-and-a-half. I soon had enough money to attend Penn State (with Mom and Dad matching my savings dollar for dollar).

By the summer of 1966, the war was in full bloom. My parents would sit down and watch Walter Cronkite deliver the news on television, fretting over reports from the war zone and worrying about their No. 3 son's draft status. They had good reason to worry. The induction age seemed to be falling every month. By the time I reached Penn State in late September, LBJ was sending off draft letters to kids who were 19 years, 3 months old – exactly my age.

"You got your draft letter in the mail," Mom said over the phone a few days after I had settled in at Penn State. "But you don't have to worry. The letter says you have a one-year deferment!"

"Read it to me, Mom."

"It says if you have begun regularly scheduled classes by the date of this notice, you have a one-year deferment."

"Mom … I'm still in Orientation Week. Classes begin next week."

Soon I was back down at the Bristol Draft Board, staring across a table at the same white-haired man who had questioned my intentions when I signed up 17 days after turning 18.

"Permission for a one-year deferment denied," he said, stamping my draft notice after a short consultation with other members of the draft board.

And off I went to the Army. College would have to wait. I was too young and dumb as a teenager to protest the war. Vietnam would wise me up in a hurry.

Induction ceremonies served as a rude awakening for approximately 150 draftees who filled the room on North Broad Street in Philadelphia. After we spent several hours walking around in our underwear, enduring examinations of various body parts by the medical staff, an Army sergeant called the guys who had passed the exam to attention and then made us stand in rows of 12.

"Recruits," the sergeant called out. "Count off 1-2-3-4 in each row." We obliged, wondering what this game would prove.

"All 4s take a step forward," the sergeant added, before pausing ever so slightly. "You are now members of the United States Marine Corps." A visible gasp went through the room. It was a historic "Holy Shit" moment, the first of many over the next two years for us former civilians.

"Did that just happen?" the guy next to me said. He had drawn the unlucky number 4. (I drew a 3 and was feeling pretty lucky all of a sudden.)

Before I could answer, the recruits were ordered back into formation.

"Get your clothes on and report back here in 10 minutes," the sergeant said. "It's time to make your induction into the United States Armed Forces official."

CHAPTER TWO:
FROM CITIZEN TO SOLDIER

HE TROOP TRAIN DOWN TO Fort Jackson, S.C. backed right up into the Army camp, delivering a collection of draftees and enlisted soldiers fresh from the streets of towns and cities all over the Northeast.

I had grown up in a lily-white suburb of Philadelphia. My sheltered upbringing hardly served as good preparation for basic training. Half of my unit was comprised of Black and Italian teenagers from New York and Philly, young men who were street-wise and smart in ways that made them seem way more confident than blue-collar suburbanites like myself.

Drill sergeants started harassing the "city slickers" right away, knowing these were the toughest nuts to crack. New York City recruits got it the worst. None of the Army "lifers" liked New Yorkers. Many of these men were career soldiers from the South who carried with them a litany of prejudices that knew no bounds. Race was the least of their concerns. They despised wise guys and malingerers more than anything. They didn't seem to like any of us new recruits.

The only exposure most of us had to military life came from the popular television show "Gomer Pyle," starring Jim Nabors as a likeable goofball private in the Marines who was constantly harassed by his frustrated boss, Sgt. Carter. We soon found that Gomer Pyle had nothing to do with real-life basic training. There was little to laugh during those first few weeks in the Army.

Basic training served as a lab experiment for non-commissioned officers, who handled waves of recruits for eight weeks at a time, chiseling away their individualistic civilian tendencies and shaping them into soldiers who would follow orders at all costs. On the first day of training, we were marched into a barber's office to have our hair shaved off, a shocking form of discipline whose purpose was to strip away our individuality so that the Army could mold us into "fighting men."

We trainees had a common enemy – these hardened drill instructors who planned to work and scare us into top physical condition over the next eight weeks.

"You recruits better get serious," Sgt. Velez would sneer at us, "because if you don't, Charlie's going to crawl out of his tunnel and slice your throat open over there in 'Nam."

Velez had already been to Vietnam as an "adviser" to the South Vietnamese Army. He respected the Viet Cong (Charlie) as any fighting man would a cunning enemy. The veteran sergeant had fought in the Korean War. He saw us as babies heading to a slaughter unless we learned how to become effective combat soldiers who worked together as a unit.

"You'll wish you listened to me when Charlie is overrunning your base camp some night," Velez screamed at us during a hand-to-hand combat exercise. Few recruits took this particular form of training to heart. We figured if the combat got to hand-to-hand, we're all dead anyway. That's how civilians think until the Army turns them into trained killers after four months of combat training.

During basic training, the Army hands out various training aids to soldiers, including a card that listed the basic tenets of "Rogers' Rangers," a Revolutionary War militia unit that perfected a form of guerilla warfare the Viet Cong had been fine-tuning in their home country for the past 20 years.

One of the wise guys in our unit couldn't resist asking Sgt. Velez about Major Robert Rogers and his Rangers. We were shining our boots in the barracks, preparing for an inspection, and the "top sergeant" was showing off his human side to us, even taking questions, something that didn't happen often during basic training.

"Aren't the Viet Cong fighting for their country the way Rogers and his men did back in the Revolutionary War?"

"No, dumb ass, they're not," Velez responded. "We're fighting to keep the North Vietnamese from taking over South Vietnam."

"Well, isn't Vietnam really just one country?"

"Shut the hell up and get back to training," Velez demanded, rising from his sitting position and staring the recruit right in the face. "What are you, a fucking hippy?"

End of discussion.

You don't flunk out of basic training. The true screw-ups would volunteer for sick call with a litany of ailments that might afflict 19-year-olds in moments of duress. Some were legit. Leg and foot injuries led the list of complaints. The drill sergeants were marching us several miles each day in combat boots, footwear we had never worn before. Blisters were common. Most soldiers tried to fight their way through these issues. Some saw sick call as a way out of the hard work. And that laid them open to abuse from the non-commissioned officers (career enlisted men) who handled most of the training.

We had one soldier who went on sick call for emotional reasons. He was a blond-haired kid from New Jersey whose name I have forgotten over the years because he was with us for such a short time. The city slickers had been picking on this kid in the showers, harassing him with taunts that I had never heard before.

"Gay boy," they would yell at him in the shower. "Go shower in the corner. Stay the fuck away from us."

My ears must have been full of soap the first time I heard this kind of bullying.

"What's a 'gray boy?' " I asked Philadelphian Walter Lister.

"Gray boy?" Lister said, looking at me with disdain. "You mean gay boy."

"Yeah, what's that?"

Lister rolled his eyes.

"Man, you don't know nothing, do you? Gay boys are homos. Fags. Queers. Now do you get it?"

"Oh … how do you know he's one of them?"

"Man, he was just staring at us in the shower the wrong way. Didn't you see him?" Lister asked.

"Just looks like another scared recruit to me," I said.

"Well, he isn't." And with that, Walter Lister walked away.

I was familiar with the terms "queer" and "homosexual," but it wasn't something that came up very often back home in the suburbs. Once again, the city kids were showing their more advanced knowledge of the real world. Or maybe they were just jumping to the wrong conclusion. This was my first experience with homosexuality, real or imagined. Like everyone else in the company, I did nothing to stop the bullying. It continued for the first few weeks of basic training. The bullies just would not leave this fragile New Jersey kid alone.

One night, we were awakened by some screaming and cursing. Lister had gone to the bathroom and found the "gay boy" laying in a pool of blood in the shower, his wrists slashed by a razor blade that he still held in his hands. This young man was going home, out of the Army. Dishonorably discharged. We saw him the next day, packing his duffel bag in the barracks, acknowledging nobody, his wrists wrapped in gauze.

Corporal Brock, a Vietnam veteran, talked quietly about this incident a few days later.

"The fastest way out of this man's army," he said, "is homosexuality. The brass fears having a homo in a unit more than a sneak attack by the enemy. They don't know what to do with the fags. It's just a plain fact. The sad part of this is, that kid could have been a good soldier. He had a good eye on the rifle range. He might have qualified as an expert. Some of you guys wouldn't let him have the chance. And the rest of you wouldn't stand up for him. That's even worse. You are going to have to have each other's backs when you get to Vietnam. You can't go picking on guys because one day that guy might be the soldier who saves your life."

Brock was right. None of us were brave enough to stop the bullying. Maybe it was the shaved heads that took away our sense of right and wrong. The Army was molding us into wolves who would faithfully follow the pack leader.

In the fifth week of basic training, knowing we were all headed to the infantry, I applied to take the officer candidate test, even though I had scored poorly on the draft board's IQ exam.

"Doesn't matter what your IQ score is," a helpful Lieutenant told me. "Just take the test. Anything that can get you out of the infantry is worth the shot."

I passed the test and qualified for the artillery's Officers Candidate School in Fort Sill, Oklahoma. When basic training ended three weeks later, most of my unit shipped off to Fort Polk, Louisiana, for advanced infantry training. I boarded a plane for Oklahoma, carrying Truman Capote's book "In Cold Blood," which seemed like a fitting read for a teenager heading off to war.

Oklahoma in January did not evoke many memories of Shirley Jones and Gordon McRae dancing and singing their way across the prairie. The wind did come howling in off the plain, that's for sure. I settled into an academic atmosphere at Artillery School, learning how to read maps, plot targets, and determine firing data for the big guns.

On weekends, the more rambunctious trainees would head to nearby Lawton for beer, music and a disappointing look at the kind of women who take an interest in young soldiers in Army towns. A black soldier named Mitch Williams from Los Angeles fit right in with the group. He turned us on to the music of Sam and Dave, who had just hit it big with "Hold On, I'm Coming."

At 21 and coming from L.A., Mitch had experienced more of life than his fellow trainees, many of whom were still 19 years old. And, he was only in the Army for six months.

"I joined the National Guard," Mitch told us. "Gonna be in this Army for six months, then serve two weeks a year for six years. I am what you would call a 'Weekend Warrior.' This nigger is NG (National Guard) all the way. You white boys can go off and be heroes."

Mitch had flunked out of college after his sophomore year, requiring him to deal with the draft before joining the Guard. His thinking on the Vietnam War was much more advanced than my own.

"Think about it," Mitch said to me one night back at the barracks. "I'm looking out for Number One. The most important person in my world is me. If you come home in a box, who's going to give a damn? Your parents, and maybe a few friends, who will go on with their lives in about two weeks and forget you ever existed. Some of them might bring your name up at a class reunion as 'the kid who got killed in Vietnam.' Poor sucker got his ass drafted out of college. In Orientation Week. Damn."

Mitch did not escape harassment from his fellow artillery trainees during our eight-week training course at Fort Sill. He had two things going against him. He was a black man in an otherwise all-white training unit. And he was a National Guardsman. "NGs" were the envy of soldiers drafted for two years, or of enlisted men slated to serve at least three years. We all resented NGs. They had played the system to good advantage, finding their way into the reserves, often with help of their local congressman.

"Not me," Mitch said. "My National Guard unit was short of black people. Can you dig it? In LA, they couldn't find any black men who wanted to join the reserves. I happened to walk in on the right day, I guess. Timing is everything."

Mitch's skin color proved a problem for some soldiers. A big, strapping kid from Kentucky named Paul Hodgson had been appointed platoon leader, even though he was a private, just like the rest of us. Hodgson tried to use his new-found power in many ways. He would demand that all of us meet various inspection standards, from shined boots and polished belt buckles, to well-made beds and starched fatigues.

None of us liked to be pushed around by another private, least of all Mitch.

Hodgson often singled out Mitch for criticism. Things took a turn for the worse the day he called Mitch "boy."

"Don't ever call me that word again, Hodgson," Mitch said, spitting the words out. "I am a man. I'm 21 years old and in the Army. I don't have to take shit from no white honky from Kentucky."

The two soldiers were soon rolling on the concrete floor of the barracks, exchanging punches, before a few of us stepped in to separate them.

"What's going on here?" said our staff sergeant, poking his head out of his sleeping quarters.

"Nothing, nothing at all," Hodgson said.

"Good. Nothing is a good thing for you guys to be doing. Now get out there in formation. We're going to have a roll call."

It was 25 degrees outside and the wind was howling across the parade ground outside our barracks. We stood in formation for 20 minutes before the staff sergeant figured we had learned our lesson. And it worked. Hodgson backed off the rest of us and never said another word to Mitch until graduation day.

"Now you're out of the real Army and going home," Hodgson told Mitch after the ceremony ended. "And the rest of us are going to Vietnam. Fucking National Guardsmen. You can all go to hell." Mitch just smiled and packed his duffel bag. He was heading home.

I asked Hodgson one night why he joined the Army.

"My dad fought in the Pacific in World War II," he said. "He told me the Japs would have taken over Australia if we hadn't stopped them. Now he says the same thing is going to happen if we don't stop the Commies in Vietnam. They'll go after the Aussies next."

"You really believe that?" I said. "Australia's a long way from Vietnam."

"The Commies are all over the place," he said. "They have spies in Australia right now."

"Interesting," I said, not choosing to prolong this discussion, and not even sure who was right. It was good to discuss things with people from other parts of the country. I was still 19 years old and forming my own opinions on the world. It seemed like soldiers from the Northeast were a lot more cynical about our government than soldiers from down South. That was just an early observation on my part, one that would be reinforced over the next 18 months. Southern soldiers were more patriotic. Almost without exception, they handled their rifles better. They were good soldiers, guys you wanted to go to war with, assuming you had to go to war.

Mitch went home to LA after Artillery School ended. We never heard from him again. That was becoming a pattern in this man's army. Every eight weeks, you made new friends, and every eight weeks the Army sent us all scattering in different directions.

I got some great advice from an officer midway through my training and dropped out of OCS, landing in a fallback artillery job called "Fire Direction Specialist," which would have me working in a section of the artillery called FDC, short for fire direction center.

"You don't want to go to Vietnam as an artillery officer," one of the class instructors, another Vietnam vet, told me. "They become forward observers and either travel with the infantry or fly in small planes above the battles. Their average life span in 'Nam is around 28 days. Best move you can make is drop out of OCS and fall into FDC. You've already been trained for that job."

Following his instructions, I soon found myself in Colorado Springs at Fort Carson, biding my time until Vietnam came calling. It was the spring of 1967.

CHAPTER THREE: NEXT STOP ... VIETNAM

WHILE MITCH WILLIAMS HAD BEEN the first to talk about the importance of self-preservation, heavyweight champion Muhammad Ali provided the starkest example yet of looking out for one's own self, and minding your own business, when he refused to step forward for his scheduled induction into the U.S. Army on April 28, 1967.

"I ain't got no quarrel with them Viet Cong," Ali had said, famously, after his Louisville draft board reclassified him from 1-Y to 1-A. True to his word, Ali would not join the Army. He would later apply for Conscientious Objector status, eventually taking his case all the way to the Supreme Court, where he was exonerated in 1970.

Few people could divide the country the way Ali did. White people resented his rambling speeches on separatism between the races. But he did speak to disgruntled soldiers of all races when it came to fighting this war in a far-off country halfway around the world.

"No, I am not going 10,000 miles to help murder, kill, and burn other people to simply help continue the domination of white slave masters over dark people the world over. This is the day and age when such evil injustice must come to an end," Ali, a convert to Islam, said.

The heavyweight champ spoke for many younger soldiers, especially draftees. Most of us were from the middle and lower classes of American life. We all had something in our lives to complain about. Ali was just voicing one of our concerns. He was using his own very public forum to speak out against a controversial war.

It shows how much the thinking in our country had changed since World War II. The heavyweight champion back then was a popular African American named Joe Louis, who had struck a great psychological blow for the free world when he knocked out Germany's Max Schmeling in the first round of their fight in 1938. When the United States entered the war in late 1941, Louis was one of the first famous athletes to enlist in the Army. He served nearly four years, boxing exhibitions for the troops while quietly working behind the scenes to cheer up Negro soldiers, as they were known in those days, men of color who were fighting in an almost totally segregated Army.

After the war, Louis found himself at odds over finances with the Internal Revenue Service, which took more than one million dollars out of his pocket, mostly in interest penalties, before backing off in the early 1960s. Although Ali and Louis were two very different people, the younger champion couldn't help but notice how badly Louis had been treated by his government after joining the Army and giving up four prime years in his boxing life.

Plenty of Vietnam-era soldiers understood Ali's motivation for not stepping forward, and were happy that he was taking on such a heavy burden, even if it did cost him three years of his boxing career, a penalty we all paid because there was no athlete more fun to watch compete than Muhammad Ali.

When our Fort Carson artillery battery lined up in formation at lunch time on April 28, the unit's First Sergeant went through his usual list of mundane announcements before concluding with a personal statement.

"Men, the heavyweight champion of the world refused to join the Army this morning," the Top Sergeant told us. "That makes him a coward in my book. You men are the heroes for stepping forward to preserve America's freedom against those bastard Communists over in Vietnam."

Very few of us were buying it. We broke formation a few minutes later and went to our work places, talking about the heavyweight champ and what his actions meant to us. Ali didn't win total endorsement from the troops, of course. Many white soldiers saw Ali as a threat to their own well-being.

Tensions between white and black soldiers in the Army were already festering back in 1967, a full year before Martin Luther King was assassinated. And this was just in a stateside military base. Vietnam would be worse.

Rumors floated through Fort Carson every week about deployments to Vietnam, either for full units or individual placements. I got my orders in late July. Take a month of leave, then report to Oakland in late August, catch a plane ride to Vietnam. The inevitable had finally come to pass, less than 10 months after I reported to Penn State for Orientation Week.

I went home to prepare my parents for the worst. Tim had just completed his four years in the Air Force. Dan, 25, had enlisted in the Army after the Selective Service decided to chase him in his last year of draft eligibility. Youngest brother Larry was only 17 years old and wouldn't face his draft crisis for another two years.

We posed for a picture in the front yard. I have retained the original Polaroid that shows four boys lined up with their dad, three of them in uniform. Dad had a big smile on his face. He still believed in what our government was doing in Vietnam, although even his point of view would change over the next year. The Tet Offensive in late January of 1968 would change the minds of many middle-aged Americans, even someone as influential as CBS network news anchor Walter Cronkite.

When it came time to leave for Oakland, my father was in the hospital following gall bladder surgery. We were both too choked up to say much. I just sat in the room with him for an hour, watching the Phillies on television and talking baseball. Finally, I got up, put my hand on his shoulder and promised, through my tears, and his, that I would see him in a year.

Tim took me to the Philadelphia airport. The last song playing on the radio as he dropped me off was "Soldier Boy." You can't make that stuff up.

They weren't singing soulful songs at the San Francisco airport. Anti-war protestors held up signs in the terminal, advising soldiers of locations where lawyers could help them avoid Vietnam. It was a little late for that. I hadn't even thought of the Canada option.

"Don't do anything to embarrass your mother" was a code of conduct our father advised us to live by in our youthful days. Truth is, Mom and Dad would have supported whatever stand their sons took. I was just too young and naïve (and scared) to make a stand in the summer of 1967.

Uncle Sam had two ways to get his soldiers over to Vietnam – slow transport ship or commercial jet. I got lucky and flew on a big plane, replete with perky stewardesses who put up a brave front and served all these young men with their usual smiles. It couldn't have been easy for them, either, knowing many of these young soldiers would never come home alive, or in one piece, or even ever the same.

We flew into Bien Hoa Airport on the outskirts of Saigon on a steaming hot day. My Army records say it was September 2, 1967. I got assigned to "A" Battery, a 2/32 Artillery unit stationed in Cu Chi, about 28 miles northwest of Saigon. We were attached to the 25th Infantry Division and would be firing missions in support of infantry units out in the bush.

The processing clerk delivered my orders and told me to head over to the motor pool, where I could hitch a ride to Cu Chi. It was all pretty informal. We were hitching rides in Vietnam instead of across town back in the USA. After watching war reports on television for several years, it felt surreal to be moving around this strange new country.

There were three of us heading to Cu Chi. We climbed into the back of a ¾-ton truck, set our gear down, and settled back for a ride into the magical mystery world of Vietnam.

Five miles into the trip, heading through a small village littered with farm animals, we spotted an Esso gas station. That was weird. It was also the first evidence that war is big business, and global. And when we stopped at a road side market, Vietnamese children raced over to the truck, trying to sell us bottles of Coca-Cola.

"It's like we never left home," one of my fellow soldiers joked.

"Yeah, this looks a lot like my home country in Georgia," the other soldier added. We would hear that line many times over the next year. With its lush green forests, Vietnam did look like the lusher, swampier parts of the USA.

Upon our arrival in Cu Chi, we sat down in the waiting area with several soldiers who had just completed their one-year tour of Vietnam and were heading home.

"Short," one of them yelled. "One fucking day left in this shithole. Taking the Freedom Bird back home tomorrow."

Then they spotted us.

"Hey, new guy, how many days you have left?"

"364," I said, to instant howls of laughter.

"Did you sign up or get drafted?"

"Drafted."

"Well, at least you didn't volunteer."

They became civil as we sat together for more than two hours, waiting to move out.

"Should we tell them about the officer in our unit who got fragged?" The short-timers looked at each other for a few seconds, then one of them started talking.

"We had this one officer who kept volunteering us for dangerous patrols," he said. "We warned him time and again. Some of the guys in our platoon were a little crazy. We told the officer he might piss off the wrong guy. One night, he's sleeping in his tent and somebody rolls a grenade in there and messes up the officer pretty bad."

The three combat veterans looked at each other uncomfortably.

"Just something you newcomers ought to know." And then they got up and left.

It was a helluva introduction to Vietnam. Soldiers were "fragging" their officers.

Walter Cronkite's nightly news accounts had provided a brief insight into Vietnam. Still, it was mind-boggling to witness all the sights and sounds of a war zone in real life. Everything was green except for the roads, which raised up clouds of dust in the dry season. Military vehicles clogged the roads – Jeeps, trucks, tanks, armored personnel carriers and in between were the bicycles of the Vietnamese, weaving in and out of the traffic. Helicopters and their rotor blades roared overhead. Jets streaked above the clouds. The ground would shake at night as B52s dropped their heavy bombs from 30,000 feet.

U.S. artillery batteries fired as many as 200 rounds a night at intersections of roads in the jungle, hoping to deter movement by the nocturnal enemy.

"Harassment and interdiction," they called those nighttime rounds. It was a fitting description of America's impact on this strategic country located on the lower tip of Southeast Asia.

CHAPTER FOUR:
TET CHANGES THE WAR

HE 2/32 ARTILLERY'S "A" BATTERY occupied a position on the west end of Cu Chi base camp. Work revolved around our four "big guns," 175-millimeter, self-propelled howitzers that could launch 147-pound projectiles up to 21 miles in any direction within a few minutes after receiving a fire mission. We also had the capacity to change those howitzers into 8-inch guns just by switching the barrels. The 8-inch fired 200-pound shells, with greater accuracy, to a range of approximately 14 miles.

There were 120 soldiers in "A" Battery, my home for the next year. We had eight enlisted men and one officer in the Fire Direction Center (FDC), which operated out of an APC (armored personnel carrier) when we were in the field. In base camp, we worked out of a well-fortified bunker. We were also the communications center for the battery with a radio unit that connected us to the entire battalion.

FDC personnel worked eight-hour shifts, four soldiers on duty and four off. That schedule rarely varied over the next year. One day you worked 16 hours, the next day you worked eight. If we were not plotting targets on our map of the region, we were calculating data for fire missions, or working up advance data for H&I fire missions. If the FDC work slacked off, we went outside and began filling sand bags with dirt to fortify our bunkers. Sleeping routines were irregular, at best. We were all between 19 and 23 years old and full of energy.

The battery possessed four gun crews with 12 soldiers assigned to each howitzer. The toughest part of their job was carrying heavy projectiles that weighed between 147 and 200 pounds from the ammo pit to the gun's breech (often while enduring enemy mortar fire). The crews also had to maintain the guns, making sure the tubes were clean and the engines ran smoothly.

We were the "big guns." Infantry troops respected us and welcomed our firing on the outskirts of their battles with the enemy.

A typical fire mission began with a Forward Observer calling in map coordinates on the unit radio band. We would alert the gun crews to a mission, plot the target on our map, compute firing data, and then relay that information to a gun crew radio man over our land-line phone.

The commands to the guns sounded this way:

"BATTERY ADJUST" (guns involved in the fire mission).

"AZIMUTH 3200" (direction of fire the guns will point).

"SHELL H.E." (high explosive shell).

"CHARGE 3" (powder charge necessary to reach target).

"FUSE QUICK" (point detonating).

"NUMBER TWO ONE ROUND, BATTERY ONE ROUND IN EFFECT" (method of fire ... gun number two will begin to fire and make corrections until the desired result on the target is observed. At that time all the guns in the battery would fire on the target using Gun Number Two's corrected data).

"DEFLECTION 2210" (direction placed on the gunner's Panoramic Telescope, moving the barrel, or tube of the gun, left or right in the desired direction toward the target).

"QUADRANT 448" (elevation placed on the Assistant Gunner's Range Quadrant. The tube is then raised or lowered until the desired elevation is reached).

"NUMBER TWO - FIRE!"

The Forward Observer, attached to an infantry unit or circling the target in a small plane, would watch the rounds hit and then ask us to add or subtract distance, and fire for effect. In those days, artillery guns still bracketed targets, finding the correct range after seeing where the first volley landed. By the early 1990s, advanced technology improved the process so much that "smart bombs" would find their targets on the first shot, thanks to a laser device implanted inside the shell.

The rest of "A" battery consisted of cooks, supply clerks, maintenance workers, officers and career enlisted men, who supplied most of the leadership on a daily basis. Gun crews were split down the middle, roughly half white and half black. I'm only mentioning this because riots had just occurred in the summer of 1967 back home in places like Detroit, Los Angeles and Newark, N.J., that aggravated racial tensions both in the USA and in the Army.

The Viet Cong were just a rumor during the first month of my tour. Charlie was an elusive enemy. He moved all around us, slipping in and out of villages at night, digging bombs into the roads, and harassing Cu Chi base camp with nighttime "sapper squad" raids. The VC never hit our side of the camp.

Twenty years after we returned home, a book came out called "The Tunnels of Cu Chi" that spoke of Viet Cong living underground near the base camp. They had built tunnels into the camp itself. The VC could actually pop up in the middle of Cu Chi base camp anytime they wanted, always at night, of course.

It chilled my spine, two decades later, to recall that we often walked, alone, from our FDC bunker to the sleeping quarters in the middle of the night, unaware of those tunnels, completely oblivious to the danger, half the time walking without a weapon. Not that I wasn't scared to death anyway. It was pitch dark at 3 in the morning, darker than anywhere I had ever been before. You do things when you're 20 years old that you would never consider at age 40 ... unless you were drafted and had no choice in the matter.

"Hey, if your time has come, your time has come," soldiers would say to each other. "Don't matter if you are walking the streets of your hometown or fighting Charlie hand-to-hand. If it's your time, it's your time."

FDC section chief Bill Kimball told us that Cu Chi and the surrounding "Iron Triangle" region just north of Saigon had been a hot fighting zone earlier in 1967 during Operation Junction City.

"You missed out on some fun times," he said, displaying a dry sense of humor that served him so well in Vietnam. Kimball had been in country six months when I arrived. He was still only 20 years old, same as me.

Our battery moved to Tay Ninh Base Camp, about 12 miles northwest of Cu Chi, in October. We went on several day-long field trips to a village called Trai Bi located hard on the Cambodian border, within firing range of the Ho Chi Minh Trail, which brought supplies and soldiers to South Vietnam. Of course, we could never fire on this busy military highway in the jungle. Our government didn't want to widen the war into Cambodia, triggering a response from Russia and/or China, who were both supplying North Vietnam with substantial aid.

On Dec. 8, 1967, A Battery moved to Trai Bi as part of Operation Yellowstone, setting up a field camp barely suitable for living. We slept in underground bunkers and ate C rations for six weeks, except on Christmas Day, when a hot meal was flown in from Tay Ninh. Hundreds of rats scurried through the camp, owning every inch of the place after the sun went down.

"We were sent to Trai Bi to support an IRDG (Irregular Defense Group, South Vietnam's equivalent to our National Guard)," Kimball recalled in 2012. "The IRDG was encamped just a short distance north of our position. When they moved out, the VC moved into the camp the same night and fired mortar rounds into our position. The next day, the Army engineers sent out heavy construction equipment to our position. They bulldozed and burned the IRDG camp, which was filled with trash. That's when the rats left the trash dump and overran our camp in Trai Bi."

We settled in for six weeks of random shooting into the countryside, serving as bait for a possible attack by the NVA troops running the Ho Chi Minh Trail. Infantry units could be flown into our perimeter within a half-hour's notice if the NVA took the bait. They never did.

Nobody attacked us at Trai Bi, nobody except the rats. Soldiers picked a few off with their M14 rifles during slow moments in their day. Dean Vincent, a tough Texan, would spear rats with his bayonet while Kimball shined a flashlight on the rodent.

Our battery clerk, Ken Metzgar, awakened one night to the sight of a rat sitting on his chest. Metzgar bolted straight up off his bed and knocked himself out when his head hit a four-by-four beam supporting the underground sleeping quarters.

These were the often humorous happenings that punctuated the standard boredom of life in a war zone. Like soldiers in every war since time began, we found mirth in discomfort. What else could we do?

When we weren't laughing, we spent our time filling sand bags, sleeping, working in the FDC tank, taking cold showers and eating.

"Something else you might recall," Kimball said, "is that when we first arrived at Trai Bi, our perimeter was protected on one side by IRDG forces and on the other side by Cambodian soldiers. This was a problem because Vietnamese and Cambodians hated each other. During that time, I guess you could say we had our own mini-DMZ that kept the two groups of soldiers separated."

We also got our first look at how the rapidly changing music culture back home was impacting soldiers in Vietnam.

"When the Army brought in a couple of gun units to protect our perimeter," Kimball said, "the Lieutenant in charge was a former rock band member. I know he drank whiskey because one day our Battery

Commander found an empty whiskey bottle outside the Lieutenant's bunker. The BC told him there would be no drinking inside the perimeter. The lieutenant then threatened to take his guns and his men and leave us without any Americans on the perimeter. Our BC relented."

The rock-and-roll officer posted a sign outside his bunker that read: "Lucy in the Sky with Diamonds," in honor of a drug-oriented tune by The Beatles.

It's interesting to look back on how The Beatles were changing as artists while we dealt with changes in our own lives. During my two years in the Army, The Beatles went from mop-haired kids singing simple rock-and-roll love songs to drug-addled musicians obscurely hinting at acid trips with their lyrics. Same thing happened to The Beach Boys, who stopped singing about cars and surfer girls and focused on their new album, Pet Sounds, in 1967. The times were definitely changing, as Bob Dylan had noted already.

"At the time, I didn't even know what that sign meant," Kimball said, thinking back to the Lucy billboard. He would go on to a 35-year career as a Chicago policeman. "I figured it out later." Bill's learning process was typical of most soldiers. We were all falling behind on the rapidly changing culture back home while serving our country 10,000 miles away. Some guys got "Dear John" letters from girlfriends, who were experiencing their own changes at home. We were giving up a year of our young lives ... for what?

Following the Christmas and New Year's truces arranged by diplomats from North and South Vietnam, the war began heating up. Few of us American soldiers knew that the Vietnamese Lunar New Year (Tet) would be celebrated at the end of January. Turned out, North Vietnam premier Ho Chi Minh and his military leaders were planning a holiday surprise attack that would hit 36 of the 44 province capitals in South Vietnam. Happy Lunar New Year!

General William Westmoreland, leader of the U.S. military effort in South Vietnam, was more interested in telling people back home that the war was going well. There had been a few ominous battles in 1967 that spoke to a different truth.

Typical American thinking, from President Johnson and Secretary of Defense Robert McNamara on down, suggested the U.S. and South Vietnamese armies were superior fighting forces to the VC and North Vietnamese armies and this would play out in a conventional war.

American troops, however, knew the ARVN army lacked commitment and would run at the sight of a tough battle. Westmoreland and his intelligence officers had the war correspondents fooled, or at least had kept them at bay, away from the front where the truth lurked around every corner.

Somebody must have forgotten to inform Westmoreland this was not a conventional war. Despite an agreed-upon ceasefire, the NVA came across the border from Cambodia on Jan. 30 and lit up South Vietnam with a series of nighttime attacks that continued for two weeks and would forever be remembered as "The Tet Offensive."

Televisions back home were filled with scenes of the U.S. Embassy under siege in Saigon. Tet cast a huge spotlight on Vietnam. Ordinary American citizens – like my parents – were finally making judgments on this war, instead of obediently listening to the country's politicians. Journalists began asking hard questions. Many of them went out in the field to get their answers from front-line troops instead of filing from press headquarters in Saigon.

Soldiers ambushed during Tet didn't grasp the full impact of the offensive right away. Our FDC radio network squawked through the night. We knew the shit was flying somewhere, maybe everywhere. My unit had returned to Tay Ninh on January 26. Four days later, we heard specific reports about the province capital attacks. The North Vietnamese Army and the VC decided to bypass Tay Ninh. We got orders to move to Cu Chi on Feb. 5. Our 8-inch guns would come in handy in a village just outside camp named Go Da Hau, where the VC and NVA were locked up in a series of battles with the 25th Infantry Division.

Two of the 8-inchers and half the FDC crew rumbled down the highway to Go Da Hau, where we came upon an infantry platoon resting on the side of the road.

"A" Battery Executive Officer Bill Haas left his Jeep to confer with an infantry captain. The men spoke for a minute and then Haas walked over to the FDC tank.

"You guys ever shoot direct fire before?" he asked.

"Yeah, back in the states," Bill Kimball replied.

ON THE MOVE – Driver Ken Barbian, bottom right, steers his APC down the road towards Cu Chi in early 1968. Lt. Haas, front left, and FDC chief Bill Kimball, top right, look on. Soldier at lower right is believed to be Rocco De Vincenzo. Soldier at top left could not be identified. (Carl Miller photo)

"Well," Haas said, "this isn't the states but everything else is the same. Our infantry can't enter the village until the VC bunkers are softened up." Haas waved in the general direction of the thick trees that camouflaged concrete bunkers in front of the village.

"The infantry have lost 10 KIA in two days trying to get past those bunkers," Haas said. "We need to lay down some fire on those bunkers."

"Yes, sir."

The firing data didn't take much computing. We were just going to anchor the guns, lower their sights to zero elevation, load them up and start firing, adjusting our range (if necessary) after the first rounds landed. It didn't take long to get the mission underway. We fired 100 rounds over the next two hours, stopping at intervals as infantry scouts assessed the damage through their binoculars. The cannoneers and FDC personnel had to hide behind the big guns to avoid being hit by shrapnel.

Finally, the infantry captain came over and told us to cease fire.

"There's no way any VC survived that barrage," the infantry officer said, impressed by the sight and sound of those 200-pound shells exploding against concrete bunkers.

The infantry then assaulted the bunkers, meeting immediately with heavy resistance from the enemy, who had sat out the pounding in tunnels below the bunkers. We later learned the VC even had a working hospital operating within the confines of an elaborate tunnel system that stretched for miles underground.

Our two-gun artillery unit set up its own perimeter, lest the enemy circle our position and attack from the rear. I was sitting in the FDC tank, monitoring the radio, when our First Sergeant came calling.

"PFC Nau, report to the perimeter," Sgt. Pryor ordered. "The infantry has two KIA that need to be loaded onto the Medevac chopper."

I grabbed my helmet and followed the sergeant to a point 50 feet away where two bodies lay on stretchers, each covered by ponchos. Corporal Ken Barbian was standing there, waiting for some help. Above us, the chopper hovered, kicking up dust and drowning out the war with the beating of its blades.

The wind whipped up as the chopper descended, blowing off poncho liners that covered the faces of these two dead soldiers. One had his lips pursed in a screaming position. The other's face simply was not there anymore. Both men had acquired a chalky coloring, a grayness that spoke of death.

Barbian, a slow-talking Texan, studied my reaction as we began to lift the first stretcher.

"You look like you seen a ghost," he said.

I had no words. The sight of those two dead bodies numbed me for a few minutes. They were a stark reminder of war's high stakes.

"Let's do this!" Sgt. Pryor yelled at us, and soon the two bodies were on their way back to base camp, two soldiers heading home. Two soldiers whose "time had come."

A few minutes later, Sgt. Pryor ordered me away from the FDC personnel carrier.

"Get out on the perimeter," he said. "Ain't nothing going on here."

I grabbed my weapon and trotted 20 yards, trying to stay low. A sharp whistling noise whizzed past my helmet. I saw dirt kick up in the distance. This war was getting personal now. People were shooting at me! A few minutes later, we heard an explosion near the FDC position. A rocket-propelled grenade fired by the enemy at our tank had flown a few feet too high and landed 20 yards away. Sgt. Lester Cure ran after the remnants of the RPG and collected it as a souvenir. Cure, a Korean War veteran, ran around with a smile on his face, showing everyone his prize, completely oblivious to the small arms fire that still rattled through our position.

There were several veteran NCOs in our battery who had experienced combat in Korea. Most of us young guys were getting our first taste in Go Da Hau. We were ready to answer the age-old question of soldiers in any war. How do you react when someone is shooting at you?

It was a question that kept me awake for most of the night back at Cu Chi base camp. I laid on my cot, thinking about the bullet that whizzed past my head. I could have been dead and never known it. I could have been dead if the RPG had hit our FDC tank when I was sitting in it, monitoring our unit radio network. I thought about those two dead soldiers who were not as lucky and worried about what we would run into the next day. A person could develop a pretty good sleeping disorder in Vietnam.

Bill Kimball wouldn't be going with us the next day. He had less than a week remaining on his one-year tour of Vietnam. Our unit's orders were to head south towards Saigon for an undetermined period. Suddenly, it was time for Kimball to pass the baton of FDC chief to someone else. Lt. Haas made the decision, choosing me to take over our little eight-man section. At the age of 20, I would be the ranking enlisted man in our eight-man FDC crew, responsible for maintaining the cohesive teamwork that Kimball, who was only 20 himself, made a top priority. Bill used his sense of humor to deflate the occasional tense moments. I would have to find my own leadership style over the final six months of my tour. I resolved to just work as hard as possible and lead by example, rather than words. Just like my Dad taught me.

We went back down the road to Go Da Hau the next day, expecting to see more action, but Charlie had abandoned the village and faded back into the jungle. He always liked to fight on his terms, not ours. Soon we were on our way to Saigon, just a few miles away.

CHAPTER FIVE:
STALEMATE IN VIETNAM

HAVING FUN – Specialist Fourth Class Mel Major, left, and fellow cannoneer Dan McCorkle ride one of the 175 howitzer tubes during maintenance session at French Fort in 1968. (Photo courtesy of Mel Major)

I T GOES WITHOUT SAYING THAT Tet was a game-changer for everyone involved in what once had been known as the Vietnam "conflict." We were facing a cunning enemy and now everyone knew it. Walter Cronkite stepped out of his objective journalist's skin to declare the war a "stalemate" in late February, 1968, and suggested the best thing we could do as a nation was to negotiate an "honorable peace" with the North Vietnamese.

The Paris Peace Talks began in May and soon became a joke to soldiers in Vietnam, as negotiators failed to make any progress towards a much-desired ceasefire. LBJ wouldn't stop bombing North Vietnam and Ho Chi Minh wasn't about to call off his NVA troops in the South. In fact, the only thing agreed upon in Paris during the rest of 1968 was the size and shape of the table around which the negotiators sat.

Our unit headed slowly towards Saigon in a long convoy of artillery guns, trucks and Jeeps that snaked its way through the streets of this famous city known to all as "The Pearl of the Orient." There is something thrilling about riding through the streets of a city during war, perched on top of the big guns, or riding shotgun in a half-ton APC … even if some of the Vietnamese citizens were waving their middle finger at us from the side of the road.

This was definitely the Baby Boomer Generation's war, one we were going to remember for the rest of our lives. Korea had settled into a quagmire just 15 years earlier and now Vietnam had become a stalemate. American citizens, who had exulted when World War II ended in triumph, wondered why we kept getting into wars on the other side of the world.

LBJ and his war council kept promoting the "Domino Theory," an outdated piece of logic that made me think the father of my old Oklahoma training pal, Paul Hodgson, had been promoted to Secretary of Defense. It is hard to believe how many Americans still bought into this idea. Some people understood the Aussies felt they owed their freedom in World War II to the United States and British soldiers who prevented the Japanese from taking over the entire Pacific Ocean in 1942. But the North Vietnamese seemed intent only on unifying their own country, with a little help from the Russians and Chinese, who provided weapons and other war machinery to keep the NVA operating at peak efficiency against the Americans.

While a small number of college students were burning their draft cards and protesting the war, soldiers in Vietnam were getting their own education on the hard facts of America's intervention in what many of us could now see as a civil war between North and South Vietnam. A growing number of soldiers in Vietnam were developing the brand of cynicism and anger that anti-war protestors displayed back home, though soldiers expressed themselves in blunter fashion. "FTA" written on a helmet liner stood for "Fuck the Army."

The average GI had more in common with anti-war protestors than he realized. Our lives had been uprooted by war-mongering politicians. Soldiers were giving two or three years to the government. Protestors could end up in jail for their disobedience. We were all sacrificing our freedom for Vietnam, even the kids back home who were still waiting for their draft number to come up in the lottery. Soldiers and protestors were both becoming politicized, forced to deal with issues of loyalty to country as the nation fought an unpopular war.

Our FDC section had turned over its entire personnel roster in the past six months, except for one short-timer, Rocco De Vincenzo, who was very upset when I got promoted to section chief over him. Rocco had what we now call anger-management issues. Fortunately, he rotated home in March, saving me some anxiety in a war zone where unnecessary stress could ruin our unit.

We now had two Californians in our midst – Lt. Tony Hoehner from Walnut Creek and a big, hairy fellow named Steve Nelson, who called San Francisco home. Hoehner was only 21 years old and more resembled an enlisted man than an officer. He sat around and told us funny stories about growing up in California. Nelson quickly earned the nickname "Hippy" for his offbeat point of view.

They were joined by New Jersey's Chuck (Rosey) Rosenblum, a fast-talking card player who was good with numbers, and Iowa's Jon Ringer, a college graduate who looked upon the whole combat situation with an ironic sense of humor. Ringer was 23, three years older than most of us draftees in FDC. Maturity in Vietnam was measured in terms of in-country service time. Last one in was always the new guy, regardless of age or education.

"At first, it was hard to take orders from guys younger than me," Ringer admitted many years later, "but I got over it."

Easy-going Carl Miller from Munster, Indiana, came in during January as a natural leader of the newer guys, along with serious Tom Barrett, the son of the mayor of Homestead, Pennsylvania, right up the river from Pittsburgh. This was the city where my father began his steel-working career in the 1930s. Tom and I connected quickly, sharing information on the area where I spent the first five years of my life. My father even knew the Barrett name when I mentioned Tom's arrival in a letter.

Uncle Sam made the war palatable for soldiers by instituting a one-year rotation system. You only had to spend 365 days in Vietnam and then it was over. This created all kinds of problems for the military brass. The best soldiers are the ones who have experienced combat over and over again. These were, with few exceptions, the soldiers who went home when their time was up. Very few soldiers extended their tours in Vietnam, even when an extension meant getting out of the Army a few months earlier than scheduled.

Lt. Hoehner proved to be an interesting fellow. He listed the Lakota Indians in his lineage.

"My dad was a Marine who fought at Guadalcanal," Tony admitted during the winter of 2013. "He was more German than Indian but was raised to speak Lakota by his mother and grandmother. The Lakota fought the U.S. soldiers and about a dozen other tribes, too. They were proud of their history the same way a Scotsman is proud of his clan or service. My uncle was half-Lakota, half-Irish. He fought in Burma and earned a CIB (Combat Infantryman Badge). I ended up with one, too, after I joined the infantry halfway through my tour of Vietnam. It is one of my proudest possessions."

Hoehner chafed under the limited action we saw during his first few months in country. His main duty was to read over and approve the firing data worked up by the enlisted men in the FDC.

"I tried hard to straddle the line between enlisted soldiers and officers," Hoehner recalled. "It was not easy but it was a smart thing for me to do. You were so much better at your jobs than I was. I finally learned to relax and trust you guys. Then my job got easier. I knew I was just there in the FDC bunker in case something went wrong."

In the summer of 1968, Lt. Hoehner answered a military advisory stating that officers with more than four months in Vietnam could volunteer to become infantry advisors.

"I jumped at the opportunity," he said. "I went to a school in Di An for two weeks to learn my craft: language training and local customs. The teams were called MAT (Mobile Advisory Team). Each team had two officers and three NCOs. One NCO was a medic and the others were infantry. But there was always a shortage of infantry lieutenants because of the high casualty rate.

"I went to a province in the Mekong Delta called Kien Phong. It was similar to Tay Ninh, close to the border and a major infiltration rate for the enemy. I lived in the Kien Van district in a compound within the city along with another U.S. advisory team. At least two of us would go out on operations with the ARVNs. We walked with them most of the time. Sometimes we traveled on boats or helicopters. I also went out on ambush patrols.

"Once, while on ambush, the compound got hit and the friendlies launched mortars into our position. I had to get on the radio and make them stop. I was so frightened that I had to have my NCO hold my hand while I crapped squatting on a steep hillside. In the dark.

"I did get to see more action with the infantry," Hoehner concluded. "Two memories stay with me. One time we were going through a dead VC's pockets and found his wallet. I saw that he carried letters and photos from home. I realized he was more like me than different. I have thought much about that over the years. Also, I saw one of our guys cut out the liver of a dead VC and wrap it in a plastic bag for cooking later on."

On March 19, an 8-inch platoon from A Battery convoyed to Di An, which was located 12 miles north of Saigon.

"If the VC attack Saigon, we'll be firing on the city from here," said our new Fire Direction Officer, a rotund ROTC graduate named Kevin Woodland, who wouldn't be around long.

We also had a civilian join our crew.

"I'm Jim Bowden," said the first combat reporter any of us had ever seen. "Freelance journalist at your service. Got sick of hanging around Saigon and decided to go out into the bush. Any problems?"

Nelson smiled at this fresh face in our midst.

"This is surreal," said the laid-back Californian. "You got any grass?"

"No," Bowden said, "but here's an old *Time* magazine. Seen it yet?"

Bowden held up the magazine for all to see. On the cover was a photo of dead Marines stacked on top of a personnel carrier, victims of the fighting in a place up north called Hue, where the heaviest action of the Tet Offensive had been fought. Soldiers went from one building to the next, fighting a nearly conventional battle in the streets against a North Vietnamese battalion.

"Oh, man," Hippy said, putting down the Time magazine and staring at the war correspondent. "Now we can read about the war while it happens. You sure you don't have any pot?"

Lt. Woodland contributed his own ridiculous moment, crushing a little puppy dog with his boot while rushing out to meet a helicopter carrying our battalion commander into Di An for an inspection. The heavy-footed officer looked back to see what he had done, pulled his pistol as if to shoot the writhing animal, thought better of it, then ordered a nearby private to "take care of that dog!" The private picked up a heavy plank of wood and killed the puppy with one blow as we watched from the FDC bunker in horror. Woodland was transferred out of A Battery shortly thereafter.

Our unit also had many positive moments, including the day Gen. Creighton Abrams visited after we had returned to Tay Ninh Base Camp in late March. Abrams was second in command of U.S. forces in Vietnam under William Westmoreland, and would succeed the embattled "Westy" in June of 1968.

Our new Fire Direction Officer, Lt. Richard Rodriguez, warned us one day to clean up the FDC and prepare for a major inspection.

"What's going on?" I said.

"Gen. Abrams is coming to inspect A Battery," Rodriguez admitted.

"What," Rosenblum said with mock surprise, "Westmoreland isn't available?"

Rodriguez smiled.

"You guys are too young to know who Abrams is," he said. "In World War II, George Patton called Creighton Abrams the best tank commander in the world, better even than Patton himself. Abrams led the relief of Bastogne. His tank unit broke through German lines and helped us win the Battle of the Bulge."

We were scheduled to shoot a Time On Target mission the next afternoon and sure enough, Abrams arrived just in time. TOT missions combined the firepower of several artillery batteries at Tay Ninh. We staggered our firing order so that the first round of volleys would all land on the target at the same time.

"What is the mission's target?" Abrams asked Rodriguez as soon as he walked into our bunker.

"It's a NVA base camp … right here," Rodriguez said, placing his finger on the map at grid coordinates that placed the target within 500 yards of the Cambodian border, just inside Vietnam.

"Okay," Abrams said. "Let's make it a good mission."

HANGING OUT – Carl Miller, right, enjoys a laugh with Terry Nau while off-duty in Vietnam. (Photo courtesy of Carl Miller)

We already had the firing data worked up. The mission was coordinated to begin promptly at 1 p.m. Our gun crews had been apprised of their needs, size of powder charge, etc. Rosey got on the phone 10 minutes ahead of the mission time with firing data, including direction and elevation of the gun tubes.

With two minutes to go, our phone line to the guns suddenly went down. Rosey threw up his hands in frustration.

"Shit," I muttered, as precious seconds slipped off the clock. I had been holding a stopwatch and knew exactly when we needed to fire our guns. The only thing I could think to do was run out to the guns myself and deliver the firing signal with a wave of my arm. Off I went, covering 25 yards to the guns in five seconds, all the while keeping time in my head. We had 20 seconds left when I got in sight of the two cannoneers holding lanyards to fire the big guns. I stopped, pointed to my eyes with both fingers, then to the stopwatch. I stuck an index finger in the air. Five seconds later, I raised my left arm slowly, then dropped it when the stopwatch hit zero. The two guns we were using on this mission fired instantly, right over my head, jolting my senses for a moment before I recovered and rushed back to the FDC bunker, where everyone was waiting for the Forward Observer circling the target in a small plane to relay results of the first round of shells.

"Hercules five-niner," came the FO's radio call. "This is Eagle one-three. Add 50 yards and fire for effect." We computed new data and again I ran out to the guns, this time asking them to raise their tubes ever so slightly and fire for effect.

When the mission was over 10 minutes later, the FO reported our rounds had landed on the target. After the infantry arrived a half-hour later, we were told that blood trails and body parts were found in the area, though not of a major amount. The NVA had gone underground to their tunnels once again.

General Abrams seemed pleased with our efforts.

"When equipment malfunctions, soldiers have to respond quickly," Abrams told Rodriguez. "Your FDC unit's training kicked in. Your men did the right thing." He saluted the junior officer and left, following his entourage to a waiting convoy of Jeeps.

We all sighed with relief after the general departed, Rodriguez most of all. The mission was good for the confidence of our young FDC unit. I had only been in charge for six weeks. Rodriguez had been with us for just two. Now we had the kind of self-confidence and respect for each other that would serve us well over the final six months of my tour.

FDC got its first exposure to computers in March of 1968. The Army sent me and Ken Barbian to a two-day school in Di An, where we learned how to compute firing data on a mobile computer unit that weighed around 20 pounds and stood on four legs. They called it "FADAC." When we got back to our unit, two of the FDC guys would work up "manual" data and another would do likewise on FADAC. If the data was close enough, we used the computer's numbers. We were all skeptics at first and I don't think we ever learned to trust that computer over our manual data.

In early April, news from back home shocked us all. We heard over Armed Forces Radio that Martin Luther King Jr. had been assassinated in Memphis. This created even more tension among soldiers all over South Vietnam.

I had become friends with a black cannoneer from Alabama, Corporal Byrd, over the first six months of my tour. Byrd was one of those people who would talk to anyone. He was easy-going and an interesting person when you got to know him.

"Blacks should be home fighting for our rights as citizens," Byrd told me after King was murdered. "Instead, we're over here fighting a white man's racist war against a bunch of Asians. When we get home, we go back to the same place we were in before we left. I know because my brother has already been to Vietnam and back. It makes no difference to white people in Alabama whether you fought in Vietnam. You're just a nigger to most of them."

I thought back to my childhood in the mid-1950s. When a black family tried to move into a home in Levittown, Pa., one town over from my hometown, they were met with rock-throwing racists who harassed them until the newcomers moved out. The actions of a few ignorant people reflected badly on the community as a whole.

"We don't want colored people moving in and driving our property values down," agitated citizens told the local newspaper. This created a moral dilemma for my parents, who had taught us to treat everyone the way we wanted to be treated. That commandment didn't extend very far in the suburbs of Philadelphia back in the 1950s. Things got a little bit better over the next decade.

At Pennsbury High, my school, we had five blacks in a senior class of 735 students. I once asked one, a star athlete named Doug Powell, to walk back to my neighborhood after school for a pickup basketball game. Doug, who lived in nearby Morrisville, which was in fact integrated, just smiled and said "no way."

I never realized until much later that Doug knew a black kid walking down a suburban street would stick out like a sore thumb. That thought had never occurred to me. It wasn't that we had a lot of racist parents or teenagers in our community. Most parents put aside their personal views to raise their children the "right" way. But it would only take one or two fear-mongering people to create a problem.

There was no open racism in my high school. We went home after school and watched the Civil Rights movement unfold on our television sets. It was natural for impressionable white teen-agers to side with the black protestors we saw on the newscasts being beaten by policemen, battered by powerful fireman's hoses, and bitten by police dogs.

Levittown and Fairless Hills both became integrated communities during the 1960s. Older whites and blacks weren't fully accepting each other yet. They cringed when white and black kids mingled together. Heck, our parents were still asking our white friends which nationality they claimed. Even my Dad used words like "Hunky" and "Polack" to describe Hungarian and Polish co-workers and friends. They all did it to one another, kidding about their ethnicity or religion. In today's politically correct world, they would be considered racists. In their world, they all got along.

Vietnam was the first place where I got to sit down and have a real conversation with the one or two black people who would talk to me. Living in a unit with soldiers from all over the USA provided many chances to learn, assuming any of us had the time to talk.

I was still 20 years old on the calendar, but it felt like we were all growing older faster. Our teenage years seemed a distant memory, thanks to Vietnam. We were no longer protected by the suburbs, or our parents. Black soldiers from inner cities across America were walking around our base camp, angry about one thing or another. Some broke the tension with humor. Others just glared at you, questioning why those FDC guys rarely hung out with the real troops. Blacks and whites had a wall between them in our battery.

In early June, another political assassination rocked us. Bobby Kennedy, brother of the assassinated president, was gunned down in Los Angeles after winning the California primary.

"Well, now we're even," Byrd said when I ran across him at the mess tent. "I don't really mean it that way, you know. But it does tell my black brothers that the world back home is getting crazier than ever. They're killing good white men, too."

Somehow, we all managed to get along during the spring and summer of 1968 while cities back home burned over racial divides. Here we were, more than 100 soldiers sleeping in bunkers protected by layers of sand bags, dodging mortar rounds from the VC at odd hours of the day and night, battling over perceived racial slights, and still hanging together to shoot our 200 rounds in a fast and efficient manner.

How did we do it? Well, it started with people like our new supply clerk, a curly-haired Irishman from New York named Kevin Dugan, who boldly joined the pickup basketball game that usually formed in the middle of camp on slow days, when it wasn't raining. Dugan broke the color line in the afternoon pickup game. It was filled mostly with black cannoneers who played a tough, physical game, pounding on one another, calling their own fouls, nearly coming to blows every five minutes.

Into this game came Dugan, who had no fear of anyone and would take the ball to the hoop almost every time he touched it. At first, his aggressive tactics aroused anger from his opponents, but he soon gained their respect.

"This is the way we play back home in New York," Dugan told his opponents, most of whom came from the South. "New York players take it to the basket whenever they can."

The games would begin around 4 p.m. as the afternoon temperature dropped below 100 degrees. They would end two hours later. It was timed that way so nobody would be shooting layups when Uncle Charlie started lobbing in his 6 o'clock mortars.

"C'mon, white boy," the blacks would yell at Dugan as he dribbled the ball 15 feet from the basket. Dugan would be glaring back with a glint in his eye, looking for a lane to the hoop. He played a physical game and when he put the ball on the ground, defenders would part grudgingly, swiping at the ball as he went by.

Dugan got along with everyone in camp. As supply clerk, he handed out all kinds of equipment when the top sergeant wasn't looking, made sure the laundry got done according to specifications, and provided a running commentary on the inner workings of the camp as he went through the details of his work day.

One night – it must have been in August – Dugan asked me what I planned to do when I rotated back to the states in September. I told him college would be nice, then possibly a career in sports writing.

"College," he sighed. "I could have had a scholarship if my grades were better in high school. I'm what you call a New York player. I could hit that jumper or take it to the hoop. You haven't seen my real game out here. The court's too hard. The ball bounces every which way. The rim stinks ... this whole place stinks."

"Sports writer," Dugan added, rolling the words over in his head. "You don't even play ball."

"Players play and sports writers watch," I replied.

Dugan nodded.

"Maybe when I get back home, I'll go to a junior college and get my grades up. Then I'll go back to college. Vietnam veteran returns home and makes good."

I nodded. Home was a far-away dream for all of us. Just talking about it made things right. Time flew when you thought of home, family, girls, hot dogs, sports and all the other things we missed because Uncle Sam decided there was a war to be fought on the other side of the world.

Our unit went on the move again in mid-April, packing all of our equipment and convoying to Thu Duc and then back to Tay Ninh base camp on April 17. One week later, we swapped base camps with B Battery, taking over a new fire base called Camp Saint Barbara, just north of Nui Ba Den Mountain. We were eight miles from Tay Ninh City, alone at the edge of the jungle, positioned to fire artillery support for infantry troops fighting near the Cambodian border in the northwest corner of Tay Ninh province.

The fire base seemed fairly safe. Thanks to a liberal dosage of Agent Orange, we could see several hundred yards into the woods from our perimeter. Engineers had begun building the base in December of 1967 and had called in jet planes to kill off the dense foliage that surrounded their project. The ground outside our base looked more like a dirt parking lot than jungle.

Our little corner of the war bogged down for a while. We settled into a methodical daily routine of fire missions and construction work inside the fire base. We would launch at least 100 rounds each night and then stand by for missions called in over the radio during the day. Most of our calls came from forward observers flying over the jungle near the Cambodian border.

Bowden, the freelance writer, had returned from a short stint with an infantry patrol unit. He resuming regaling us with tales of Saigon, 14-year-old prostitutes, cheap bars, the black market and rear-echelon soldiers on perpetual leave.

"You can't cover the war from Saigon," Bowden said. "The Army holds a press conference each afternoon at 5 that is known as 'The Five

O'Clock Follies.' No matter what kind of battle is going on – Hue, for instance – they always tell us the VC suffered heavy casualties while we sustained 'minimal' losses. I wonder how anybody getting killed could be considered minimal."

Bowden enjoyed the banter with our FDC crew and even found some pot for the Hippy. He wanted to see us in action, firing a mission with casualties on the other end. He was a reporter looking for a story.

"How often do you get reported KIAs from your mission?" he asked me.

"Not too often," I found myself saying. "The VC tend to drag away their dead before the infantry can count them. If we do score a direct hit, there's nothing left to count."

"You guys are long-distance killers," Bowden said, not meaning any offense. He was right, though. We never got to see the damage we were doing and that was good because I certainly didn't have the stomach for the kind of carnal damage a heavy artillery shell might do to the enemy.

Later that afternoon, the radio static was interrupted by an air observer calling in a mission.

"Hercules five-niner, this is Lima Bravo three-eight ... fire mission."

"Here's your chance, Bowden," I said, while reaching for the radio microphone.

"This is five-niner."

"Fire mission. Coordinates X-Ray Tango 097420. Victor Charlie in the open. On a bicycle. Fire when ready."

"Roger, Lima Bravo. Coordinates X-Ray Tango 097420. Fire when ready."

Hippy and Ringer plotted the target on the big map while Rosey and I worked up firing data. Rosey alerted gun number four for a mission. The cannoneers sprang into action, lifting those heavy projectiles on to the rear of their howitzer.

Rosey then communicated his firing data to the gun's radio operator. The gun was ready to fire 30 seconds later. The gun crew's radio man repeated the firing data back to us and then received the okay to fire.

"Lima Bravo, this is five-niner. Fire, over."

Thirty-five seconds later, I told the observer to expect a "splash." The round would be landing shortly. A VC's war career hung in the balance.

"Five-niner, this is Lima Bravo. Short 50 meters. Add 50 and fire for effect."

The gun crew received its commands, adjusted the tube elevation, and slung three rounds back out into the afternoon sky.

"Lima Bravo, rounds complete. Splash in five seconds, over."

"Roger," came Lima Bravo's response a minute later. "Rounds were on target. I can see the bicycle is destroyed. Can't see Victor Charlie anywhere. I think we knocked him off the bike with the first round and he's hiding somewhere down in the bush."

"Can we have a summary of the mission, over?"

"Roger, five-niner. One fish net destroyed. One bicycle damaged. Can't give you a confirmed KIA on Victor Charlie."

Hippy suddenly started laughing.

"What's he laughing about?" Bowden asked me.

"Well, ever since I told Hippy these rounds cost $200 apiece, he has been keeping track of our personal Defense Department spending account."

"Yep," Hippy said with a laugh. "Dig this: We just spent $1,000 to destroy a fish net and damage a bicycle. And if you count the 100 rounds of H&I we fire, that's $20,000 every night."

Our battery commander, Major Ranck, soon popped into the bunker, killing the levity.

"What were we shooting at?"

"Had a VC in the open," I told him.

"Did we get him?"

"Maybe. The observer said we knocked him off his bike and destroyed his fish net."

"Good," Ranck said. "Every little bit helps." Then he spun on his heels and went back to his bunker.

Bowden smiled at the whole scene.

"It may not seem like much to you guys," he said, "but I have been with the infantry out in the bush when heavy artillery fires support. It is hard to explain the impact of those shells hitting the ground. The infantry guys love the artillery."

I nodded in agreement, for a different reason. Working in the artillery allowed me to rationalize any death and destruction we were causing in Vietnam. We never saw the effects of our shooting, never saw any dead bodies lying in the field, dismembered beyond all recognition. We were often 10 or 20 miles from where our bombs landed.

At the cost of $1,000, we had just given a VC one major headache, assuming he even was an enemy soldier. Maybe he was just a civilian heading to the local fishing pond? Maybe he was just a messenger boy delivering some information to the local VC platoon?

These were questions we didn't spend much time pondering during our year in Vietnam. Later on in life, there would be time to consider the morality of our actions back when we worked for Uncle Sam's war machine.

CHAPTER SIX:
"WE GOTTA GET OUT OF THIS PLACE"

BOMBS AWAY – Clouds of smoke from a B52 bombing run appear on the horizon at French Fort, also known as Camp St. Barbara, in the summer of 1968. (Photo courtesy of Larry Kleinschmidt)

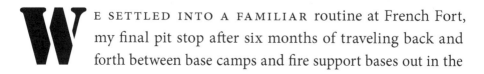

E SETTLED INTO A FAMILIAR routine at French Fort, my final pit stop after six months of traveling back and forth between base camps and fire support bases out in the countryside. The top of Nui Ba Den, a large hill known as the "Black Virgin Mountain" to locals, was visible on most days from French Fort. This was where Special Forces and the 125th Signal Battalion had set up a radio relay station on top of the 3,000-foot peak.

We could see helicopters dropping off supplies on top of the hill almost every day.

"The Vietcong control the bottom two-thirds of the Black Virgin Mountain," Major Ranck told us. "Special Forces have set up strong perimeter security around their camp at the peak."

"What happens if they get attacked?" someone asked the battery commander.

"They can chopper in relief troops from Tay Ninh Base Camp," Ranck said. "Artillery can fire support from Tay Ninh, but we won't be able to support them from here. If our rounds go long, they would clear the mountain and possibly land in Tay Ninh City."

The North Vietnamese Army and Viet Cong had bypassed Tay Ninh Province during the Tet Offensive. As April turned into May, though, intelligence reports began to warn of renewed interest in our little corner of the war. Mortar attacks on French Fort came more frequently, often around 6 in the evening as soldiers took their showers at the end of the day. The road to Tay Ninh turned up a few more land mines, explosives the local VC found time to plant during nighttime hours when they roamed without fear of retribution.

Finally, on May 13, all hell broke loose on top of Nui Ba Den. We heard the unit's first frantic plea for help at 10:30 in the evening.

"We need artillery support ASAP," came a static-enshrouded voice over the battalion radio network. That was all we heard before losing contact.

Jon Ringer came running into the FDC bunker, out of breath.

"You should see the fireworks on top of the mountain," he gasped. "It looks like they're being attacked."

All of us working that night went outside to take a look. Nearly everyone in the battery was up and moving around, spell-bound by the light show two miles away, 3,000 feet above ground.

"Everyone take their positions on the perimeter!" Gunnery Sgt. Bolden yelled at his cannoneers. "We could be in for some shit, too."

Few people in A Battery got any sleep that night. The deadly firefight on top of the mountain lasted for around two hours before giving way to the orange glow of burning embers. In the morning, relief helicopters showed up to carry off the dead and wounded. It had been too dark and dangerous for the choppers to intervene after the first radio call went out at 10:30 the previous evening.

We learned a few days later that 24 Americans died and 35 were wounded on that little signal station. It was a heavy price to pay for possession of a radio tower.

Our own perimeter security got a lot tighter after May 13. Still, many of our soldiers continued to visit the trash dump outside our front gate each day, looking to barter for cigarettes, beer and sex with the villagers who set up shop nearby.

Sex was a constant topic of conversation all over the battery. Most of us looked forward to having a good time on the one-week R&R (rest and relaxation) vacation the Army granted us at some point in our Vietnam tour. We could imagine having a good time while listening to Armed Forces Network, which had a few sensual female voices on the air as disc jockeys. And every once in a great while, the Special Services branch of the Army would bring in a traveling show of dancers, musicians and comedians to remind us of home.

Bob Hope never got deep enough into the bush to see us. The great American entertainer visited all the big bases and occasionally flew into a hot spot up near the DMZ. However, Hope and Raquel Welch and Joey Heatherton were just rumors to "A" Battery, 2/32 Artillery.

Some of the daily stuff going on outside the front gate of French Fort wasn't pretty.

"I saw Sgt. Strang pulling up his pants at the trash dump,'" a cannoneer told us. "A little Vietnamese girl, maybe 13 years old, came out behind him."

"That's gross," Hippy muttered.

Strang weighed around 250 pounds, probably three times the girl's size.

"We're really doing a great job of fucking this country over," Hippy added. "We napalm their jungles, bomb their villages, screw their daughters. They're going to remember the good old USA for a long time after we finally leave this place."

Armed Forces Radio happened to pick just this moment to play one of the soldiers' favorite songs of the war, "We Gotta Get Out of This Place," by The Animals.

"We gotta get out of this place," Hippy shouted over the music coming out of the radio box. "If it's the last thing we ever do!"

We all joined in for a few verses.

"We gotta get out of this place
If it's the last thing we ever do
We gotta get out of this place
Girl, there's a better life for me and you,

Now my girl you're so young and pretty,
And one thing I know is true yeah
You'll be dead before your time is due, you know it.

Watch my daddy in bed … a-dyin'.
Watch his half bitten turnin' grey yeah
He's been work-in' and slavin' his life away I know he's been working
so hard."

There were a lot of popular songs that soldiers could twist into their own sentimental frame of reference. "Leaving on a Jet Plane" was, in our reality, an ode to soldiers unhappily leaving for Vietnam. Peter, Paul &

Mary were more famous for their anti-war songs, but this one made a lot of GIs happy.

All my bags are packed I'm ready to go
I'm standin' here outside your door
I hate to wake you up to say goodbye
But the dawn is breakin' it's early morn
The taxi's waitin' he's blowin' his horn
Already I'm so lonesome I could die

So kiss me and smile for me
Tell me that you'll wait for me
Hold me like you'll never let me go
Cause I'm leavin' on a jet plane
Don't know when I'll be back again

"The Letter" by the Boxtops spoke to our eventual homecoming, although a soldier would have to go AWOL if he abided by these words.

"Gimme a ticket for an aeroplane
I ain't got time to take a fast train. Lonely days are gone, I'm a-goin' home 'cause my baby just wrote me a letter.

I don't care how much money I gotta spend. Got to get back to my baby again. Lonely days are gone, I'm a-goin' home 'cause my baby just wrote me a letter.

Well, she wrote me a letter, said she couldn't live without me no more. Listen, mister, can't you see, I got to get back to my baby once more?

Anyway, yeah, gimme a ticket for an aeroplane. I ain't got time to take a fast train. Lonely days are gone, I'm a-goin' home 'cause my baby just wrote me a letter ..."

We all loved Motown music. There was no racial divide here. Smokey Robinson's "(I) Second That Emotion" brought out the high-pitched singing talents of many soldiers. Otis Redding's "Sitting on the Dock of the Bay" made us all melancholy. Sam & Dave's "Soul Man" got soldiers dancing, an odd sight in a war zone.

Music was the great common denominator, one of the ways soldiers of all colors connected during their tours. And many years later, certain songs popular in 1967 and 1968 would always bring back visceral memories of Vietnam, those helicopter blades bap-bap-bapping in our heads as we went back in time to when we were young men trying to survive this war zone.

When Hollywood started making movies about Vietnam in earnest, not the "Coming Home" and "Deerhunter" misfires but the real stuff, "Apocalypse Now" and "Platoon" and "Full Metal Jacket," the film people always got the music right. It was hard to get it wrong. The Doors were integral to "Apocalypse Now," a heavy metal, haunting group whose sound evoked this era, and this war, more than any other.

By August, I had finally become "short." Due to head back home on Sept. 2, I stayed busy with fire missions, sometimes spending 20 hours in the FDC bunker rather than lying awake in our sleeping quarters, which were overrun by rats on most evenings.

On a rare night when I did sleep in our quarters, the rats started gnawing on a "care package" of candy from home that I foolishly stored under my cot. They woke me up at 2 in the morning with the frenzy of their feasting, devouring Reese's Cups and cookies my mother had sent along by mail.

"Those rats never ate so well in their lives," Rosenblum said while shining his flashlight at the scene underneath my cot.

Ringer, the college graduate, hated rats and would not sleep in his rack at night. He moved his stuff into the FDC bunker and only visited our sleeping area during daytime hours.

Rats showed up in the strangest places. One day I was taking a dump in the outhouse. This involved sitting on wooden planks that had a hole cut out for the business end of this transaction. The waste was collected in a sawed-off 55-gallon diesel fuel drum. Hordes of flies lived in those drums, along with an occasional rat. One day, something jumped up and hit my ass. It was either a horsefly or a rat. I didn't stick around to find out.

Showers were rat-free. You just had to worry about mortar attacks. The VC seemed to have a good idea when soldiers would be showering and managed to disrupt many a session with their mortar attacks. They rarely hit anything. But we all went flying out of the makeshift showers, towels wrapped around our waists as we dove for the nearest hole in the ground.

It was no wonder we all couldn't wait to return home to the warmth and safety of our homes back in the USA.

CHAPTER SEVEN: HEADING HOME

NOBODY GOES ANYWHERE IN THE army without marching orders from the bureaucracy. My orders to leave active duty came down from headquarters of the 25th Infantry Division. I was due to go home on Sept. 2 but got a pleasant surprise five days earlier when the mail arrived by chopper from Tay Ninh base camp.

"Your orders are here," the battery clerk announced during mail call, handing me the hallowed documents as fellow soldiers looked on with varying degrees of emotion. Some were happy for me. Most were jealous. "Short-timers" are mini-celebrities in camp until they're actually going home. Then they become envied.

Now that it was official, all I had to do was pack my bags and find a chopper ride back to Tay Ninh. The next one due to stop at French Fort would arrive at 11 a.m. on the following morning. I suddenly was hit with a bittersweet emotion, knowing I was leaving these new friends I had made over the past year. Soldiers only have a sense of this unbreakable connection when they are young, a vague idea that these are the guys who experienced something that not even your own brothers would understand. We shared our fears and our dreams while stepping carefully through a war zone. We understood the adrenalin that flows through our veins when somebody yells **"IN-COMING!"**

Fortunately, nobody got killed during my year with A Battery. Corporal Byrd was slightly wounded in a mortar attack three weeks before I went home. One of the previous battery clerks had blown his right hand off while test-firing a bazooka during the daily "Mad Minute" held on the camp's perimeter. Otherwise, our battery emerged almost unscathed.

Friends like Bill Kimball had gone home six months earlier. Vietnam was a war of attrition for American soldiers, who had a one-year ticket to Southeast Asia, with a return home guaranteed, dead or alive, unless you went missing in action. This is how our country decided to fight an unpopular war, by drafting citizens into the Army and promising them their duty had a time limit on it. Draftees were reluctant soldiers who grabbed the best deal they could take under the circumstances. One and done in Vietnam. This is not how the United States had fought previous wars. Draftees in WWII served for the duration.

Politicians and military strategists knew from the start that they couldn't sell Vietnam on an ever more knowledgeable population in the 1960s. Young people were more informed by television and a less loyal media. We were perhaps a bit less patriotic than the previous generation. Maybe even a lot less.

Several of the FDC guys gathered to chat and reminisce the night before I left French Fort. Half the guys were working as someone had to be monitoring the radio network. Ringer, Miller, Rosey and Barrett wished me well and told me what they would do when their time to get out of Vietnam arrived.

Armed with the hindsight of 40 years, here is how their lives turned out:

Carl would head home and become a barber, cutting hair and telling jokes back in his Indiana hometown of Munster. Rosey returned to New

Jersey and entered the restaurant/nightclub industry. He would host a young comedian named Eddie Murphy in the early 1980s. Ringer ended up in the newspaper business, just like me, only he would be an ad salesman, working in Morris, Ill.

Barrett returned to smoggy Homestead, Pa., in January. His father would die suddenly of a heart attack a few years later, just as my dad would die six months after I got home. Barrett would eventually become a teacher, living his life in Florida, far from the cold winters and dirty air of western Pennsylvania.

The Hippy had been transferred to a gun crew midway through the summer after screwing up a fire mission's details in front of the division commander, one of a long string of errors he made while computing firing data in a haze of smoke. He got along famously with the cannoneers and survived the war. Ringer got a letter from him, date marked Copenhagen, in the early 1970s. We never heard from The Hippy again.

Ken Barbian, who had lifted those two dead infantry soldiers onto a helicopter with me during Tet, was already home in Texas, having rotated out in early August. Ken founded his own tool-and-die company in Abilene. Ken had teamed with and was eventually replaced by Mike Neisius, a quiet Midwestern soul who owned the same type of mechanical skills as his predecessor. Ken and Mike were probably the two most important members of the FDC because they knew how to fix things. They kept our personnel carrier running, made sure the backup generator was always ready to go, and did any quick carpentry work that cropped up.

A new battery commander had taken over in early August. Captain Donald Babb was a West Point graduate who immediately endeavored to make Camp Saint Barbara's perimeter more secure. Babb felt the road leading into the camp would serve as an entry point for any full-scale attack by the VC and NVA. He requested a 105 millimeter howitzer and gun crew be assigned to the camp along with a pallet or two of flechette ammunition for the howitzer.

According to his book, "Memoirs of Major Donald Babb," the then-captain made his request straight to Gen. Walter Richardson, Deputy Commanding General, II Field Force, when the general dropped in for a visit.

Gen. Richardson asked why Babb felt he needed the gun crew and howitzer.

"For direct fire purposes," he said. "There is one easy way to get into this fire base and that is on the roadway coming straight into camp through the three fence lines. If the VC or NVA elements launch a full-scale attack, then I think they will try to breach the fences along that roadway. With a 105 howitzer and the flechette rounds, we could make them pay a heavy price."

Two days later, the deed was done. That howitzer and gun crew would come in handy when the camp came under attack on Sept. 17. Meanwhile, my timing for leaving seemed very good. I had some guilt about going home as the enemy began to target our fort out in the middle of nowhere. But I was no hero and never considered extending my tour.

Our futures were still dreams while we were stuck in Vietnam. I was leaving now and my crew was trying to feel good about it, even if they had their own doubts about how smoothly things would go once their section chief for the past six months was gone.

"You guys will be fine," I told them. "Kimball left in the middle of Tet. We all got through that together. Carl and Rosey will take over and you'll forget who I was in a few weeks."

(The real truth, which I never told them, is I was fortunate to be surrounded by conscientious FDC personnel who took pride in their work. It is the same trait I would see in them four decades later when we met for reunions and looked back on our lives. It was easy to lead this group of young soldiers. And they did do quite well without me.)

The muffled sound of mortars dropping into camp interrupted the conversation. Fortunately, we were all sitting inside our bunker, relatively safe from anything but a direct hit.

"Charlie is stepping up his schedule with the mortars," Barrett said. "Not sure if I like that at all."

I got up the next morning, finished packing my duffel bag, and waited for the chopper to Tay Ninh. Said my good-byes while feeling an exhilaration about going home that overwhelmed all of my senses. Still, there was this foreboding. You always heard sad stories about soldiers who got killed on their way out of country.

"Chopper crashed on his way back from the jungle. Poor guy. Had two days left in country."

My chopper arrived on time. I climbed aboard and looked into the faces of ARVN soldiers catching their own ride into base camp. None of them knew where I was going but they smiled anyway. It was hard not to like the Vietnamese. The young girls were beautiful. Children always had their hands out, begging for small favors from American soldiers. Adults were polite and friendly, unless they happened to be VC sympathizers.

I settled in for the night at my old base camp in Tay Ninh, recognizing a few familiar faces among the Vietnamese wait staff in the mess hall.

"Long time, no see!" an old mama-san exclaimed as she ladled some slop onto my metal dinner plate. "You going back to USA?"

"Yep," I said.

"No, Charlie going to get you tonight!" she laughed, showing off her toothless smile.

"Well, he only has one more chance," I told her. "One more night," I said, holding up a finger.

"Charlie Number One," she added, holding up a finger of her own. An index finger, fortunately.

Of course, we suspected some of the Vietnamese workers in our base camps served as double agents, measuring off distances to various buildings and ammo dumps. They were spies in our midst who worked both ends of the war, collecting money for waiting on the U.S. troops, and then delivering information to the Viet Cong for use at night. If the situations had been reversed, I probably would have done the same thing.

The next day, I boarded a short flight to Bien Hoa Air Base, located around 20 miles from Saigon. This is where the commercial airlines dropped off soldiers heading to war and picked up the lucky ones leaving the war. Dead soldiers were flown back on military transports. Survivors got to experience the happiest plane ride of their lives.

We had around 150 soldiers on the plane, all of them anxious to see this big bird get up in the air and out of Vietnam. A loud roar erupted as the plane left the runway and soared into the sky. The threat of death in a war zone evaporated into thin air. Stewardesses walked up and down the aisles, flirting with some soldiers, serving others whatever drinks they wanted. I just remember this amazing feeling of relief. I was going home after nearly two years in the Army, heading back to college at the age of 21, hoping I hadn't forgotten how to study.

We flew into Oakland, where anti-war protestors had often gathered to harass soldiers returning from Vietnam. When the plane's wheels hit the tarmac, another cheer erupted, this one from the hearts of the soldiers. Some guys changed into civvies as soon as they got into the airport. My plan was to come home in uniform for my parents' benefit, take it off at home and never wear it again. The war was over for me and I did not plan to ever look back.

Fortunately, our plane arrived late in the evening. The airport was devoid of protestors, who apparently like their sleep as much as the next guy. We walked without incident through the airport before boarding busses to the processing center. It took several hours before I was released from active duty, given mileage money, and booked on a plane to LaGuardia Airport in New York City.

Once I got my plane ticket, I made a long-distance call home, collect.

"Will you accept the charges?" I remember the operator asking my Dad. It was 4 a.m. back home in Pennsylvania.

"It will be the happiest day of my life when I do," Dad said, his voice loud and clear over the phone.

A few soldiers who sat near me on the long plane ride home decided to stay over in San Francisco and spend some of the travel money Uncle Sam had given them. They wanted to see the city, even if it was the anti-war capital of the country.

"We're just going to the topless bars," one of the guys told me. "Won't be any protestors stripping their clothes off there!"

"You guys go ahead," I said. They were all strangers to me. I just wanted to get home and see my family.

My parents were waiting at the gate when I got off the plane. They looked the same as when I had left one year earlier. I would learn through conversations with Mom how worried they both had been while watching the nightly newscasts from the war zone. It was easier for me than for them because I knew where I was. Mom had a map on the wall in the kitchen with little pins sticking out from every town and hamlet in South Vietnam that I had mentioned in my letters.

"We knew you weren't telling us everything in your letters," Dad said as we talked on the ride home from the airport.

I tried to steer the conversation away from the war but Dad wouldn't let me.

"How was the food over there?" he asked.

"The food was fucking awful," I said, lapsing into the expletive-laced conversational pattern soldiers bring home with them from the military.

Dad leaned over and glared at me.

"Son," he said, sternly, "I know you've been in a war and picked up some bad habits. But here's another rule for you. We never curse in front of your mother."

And that's when I knew I was back home again.

CHAPTER EIGHT:
CAUGHT BETWEEN TWO WORLDS

THE FIRST THING I DID when I got home was take off my uniform and jump on the scale. I weighed 147 pounds, exactly the same as when I left a year earlier, and saw that as a good sign. I would never wear the uniform again. It went back into a duffel bag and eventually got lost in the shuffle when I moved to Rhode Island in 1982.

"The war didn't change me at all," I said to myself, adopting a mantra I would repeat whenever life got me down. I didn't want to use Vietnam as an excuse for anything that went wrong.

My "little" brother Larry had grown up while I was gone. He was 18 years old now, working full-time in the steel mill's masonry department, making enough money to think about buying his own car. And he had lost his baby fat, growing into a lean 5 feet, 10 inches and 160 pounds of muscle. My days of kicking his ass were over!

"I want to join the Army when my draft number comes up," he told me on my first day home.

"Larry, you don't want to do that," I told him. "This war isn't worth it."

"But you and Tim and Danny all went into the service," Larry pointed out.

"Yeah, and three is enough from one family," I said, telling him nothing he hadn't heard already from both parents and his two oldest brothers.

Larry glanced at me for a second, then looked away. It was hard to tell what he was thinking. As the youngest brother, Larry had the toughest role in the family, following in each of his three brothers' footsteps.

"Larry," I said, "you are doing great. You got out of high school in June and already have a full-time job. You're making good money. Enjoy it. And when you turn 19 next summer, see what the draft board is doing by then. Maybe the war will be over."

Mom stepped into the conversation. "And you're still going to college, Larry."

By this point, Danny had graduated from Methodist College in North Carolina before enlisting in the Army in 1966. He had to enlist because Uncle Sam was still chasing him, at age 25, through the draft. Tim completed his Air Force tour in the early summer of 1967 and was now attending Penn State's main campus, working on a degree in labor relations. I was scheduled to attend the Ogontz branch campus of Penn State in nearby Abington, Pa., beginning in late September, three weeks after I got home from Vietnam.

Meanwhile, I had to catch up on what was going on in the neighborhood. There were friends to see. I also wanted to buy a used car with money saved during the past two years.

"Terry, you have to go up and pay your respects to Mr. and Mrs. Seanor," Mom said.

We had grown up playing sports with the Seanor brothers, Ed and Bobby. It was Bobby who had been killed at age 18 earlier in 1968 while driving his motorcycle through the streets of Newtown.

"Larry, would you come with me?"

"Sure."

The Seanor family lived six houses up the street from us. It was a short walk. I had changed out of my Army uniform and back into civilian clothes. We knocked on the door and were let into the house by Mrs. Seanor, whose eyes welled up in tears at the sight of us.

"I'm so sorry about Bobby," I said.

Mr. Seanor came into the living room, half-dressed. He had always been a bit of a character, a colorful personality who spoke easily and with humor to the neighborhood kids as we cut through his backyard to get to the baseball and football fields.

"Funny thing," he said to me. "You spend a year in Vietnam and come home alive. My Bobby buys a motorcycle and gets killed 10 miles from home."

"Abby" Seanor sat down on the couch and looked up at me and Larry.

"You know what they say," he said. "When your time has come, your time has come."

Where had I heard that line before?

A lot of my high school buddies were hard to find. Some were married and settled down in their jobs already, many of them working at the steel mill. Quite a few were finishing up their senior year in college. I was three years behind my contemporaries.

Dad and I went looking for a used car, armed with $2,000 we had saved up over the past two years. For every dollar I contributed, Mom and Dad threw in one of their own. I settled on a 1967 Pontiac Le Mans, which was one step below one of the iconic late 1960s cars – Pontiac's GTO. The Le Mans was nice enough for me and less expensive.

When the salesman asked me how I was going to pay for it, I reached in my wallet and pulled out twenty $100 bills.

"Okay," the salesman said, a little surprised by this form of payment.

"My son just got home from Vietnam," Dad said by way of explanation. "He saved all that money while he was in the Army."

The salesman wrote up a bill of sale and off we went. I took Dad and Mom for a ride later that afternoon. We drove through the back roads of

Upper Bucks County, riding up River Road, next to the Delaware River, not far from where Washington fought his big battle with the British less than 200 years earlier.

Dad had something to say.

"Son, you know your mother and I are so proud of you," he began. "We were worried from the moment you were drafted."

"Me, too," I agreed.

"And now you're a war veteran," Dad continued. "I never fought in World War II, son, but having three boys who served in the military makes up for it. We just need to get your brother Dan home before we can take it easy." (Dan would serve as a medic at Fort Lewis, Washington, tending to many casualties of war, before his tour ended in 1969. Larry would draw a high number of 313 in the 1970 draft lottery and avoid the military.)

Our family wasn't much different than many blue-collar families around the country. Working-class kids joined the Army or got drafted into it. Some people joined the Navy or the Air Force so they would have some control over what kind of military job they got.

You didn't see too many college graduates in the Army, although I did work with two – Jon Ringer and Tom Barrett. Bill Grelecki finished three years at Marquette before he dropped out temporarily and got swooped up by Uncle Sam.

"I was a much better student when I got out of the Army and went back to college," Grelecki said at the 2013 Reunion. "The Army was good for me in that regard. I was just a kid before I went in but I was serious about school after I got out of the service."

Tim had done the paperwork and got me enrolled at Penn State-Ogontz earlier in 1968. It made sense to stay close to home for at least my first year of college. My great emotional need was to get close again with my parents and reconnect with old hometown friends. I could join Tim up at the main campus in the fall of 1969, assuming all went well with my studies.

It had been more than three years since I last attended class in earnest. My three weeks at Penn State in 1966 didn't count. I had some real trepidation about becoming a student again. The three-year gap between me and the average freshman seemed huge. I was always an "old soul" who got along better with older people and now I was heading back to college, sitting next to kids fresh out of high school.

Once school started, my fears ended. I arranged an easy first-term schedule of classes. There were a few veterans on campus who wanted to hang out. After not seeing any American women for an entire year, my eyes were working overtime, adjusting to the short mini-skirts, jeans, and tee-shirts that dominated female clothing attire on a college campus.

Most of my high school friends were finishing up their senior year of college. I soon found that they had advanced far past me in the social whirl of the late 1960s. I would have to learn how to fit into my new world. It would be a bigger adjustment than I imagined while dreaming about going home from Vietnam.

Then one day in late September I got a letter from Chuck Rosenblum.

"Terry, things got very bad last week," Chuck began. "We were getting hit by mortars every day and they were finding their range in the center of camp. Some of the guys in the gun crews were catching shrapnel. Then last week we heard a loud explosion right outside the FDC bunker. Me and Ringer ran outside and saw Captain Babb laying there. His legs were soaked with blood. He had taken almost a direct hit. I think he lost both of his legs.

"You know what I did?" Rosey continued. "I threw up. I'm embarrassed to say this but it's the truth. We got a medevac called in and the captain was taken away. I don't think we're ever going to see him again."

A communications section private named Ron Nedjalik had been standing near the captain and suffered serious shrapnel wounds.

Rosey had more bad news.

"Dugan's truck ran over a mine on the road back to Tay Ninh," he said. "He took a lot of shrapnel. They operated and then flew him to Japan. I think he's hurt pretty bad."

The letter hit me hard. I thought I was over Vietnam, but suddenly knew it wouldn't be over for me until all of "my guys" had got home. Here I was, sitting in a college classroom with frivolous teenage girls giggling next to me, and soldiers I had served with just a month earlier were running for their lives in South Vietnam.

A few weeks later, Rosey sent me an update. Dugan died in Japan from a blood clot. Captain Babb had both legs amputated. The mortar attacks continued through October before things settled down. A cannoneer named Andy Bailey went home with a serious head injury that would complicate the rest of his life.

I began to realize I had very little in common with anyone save for the few veterans I had met on campus. And some of them were a little odd, wearing their Army shirts around campus, almost as though they wanted the students to know they were veterans.

Vietnam dominated the national debate as Hubert Humphrey ran against Richard Nixon in the presidential election of 1968.

"I can't vote for either of them," Dad, a lifelong Democrat, said one night as we watched the national news on television. "Humphrey wants to continue LBJ's war policy. Nixon can't be trusted. I might have to vote for George Wallace!"

Those were the choices we had in 1968. LBJ had stepped aside. The Paris Peace Talks continued to drag on without any progress. Nixon claimed he would curtail the war if he won the presidency, but who could believe Tricky Dick?

In November, I took a full-time job as a copyboy for the *Philadelphia Daily News*, figuring I could work nights at the newspaper and cram my classes into three days per week during the winter semester. My plan was a little shaky. I slept through a lot of classes that winter. But I did get a good education in how newspapers were put together.

The *Daily News* had an old-time managing editor named J. Ray Hunt whose sole duty each night seemed to revolve around how reader-friendly he could make Page One of the tabloid newspaper. One of my many menial jobs was to strip pictures off the wire-photo machine and deliver them to Mr. Hunt.

One night I showed him a photo of a very dead actress named Jayne Mansfield, who had been killed in a horrific car crash the previous summer. A gory photo shot at the scene had suddenly been made available to media outlets.

"Here it is!" Hunt said, rising out of his chair as cigar ashes flicked onto his white shirt. "This is a Page One newspaper photo." The *Daily News* sold a lot of papers the next day.

Whenever Hunt needed me, he would shout "boy" across the newsroom. "Boy, get me some copy paper." Or, "Boy, go check the newswire. Tell me what those bells are ringing for."

After a month of this, I had enough.

"Mr. Hunt," I said. "I just got out of Vietnam. Do you mind calling me something other than boy?"

Hunt looked me over, as if for the first time, and smiled.

"How about if I yell ... copy?" he said, flashing a rare smile, seemingly pleased with his solution. And so it was. "Copy" was my new name around the newsroom.

The 40-hour work week caught up with me during the winter. I would almost fall asleep driving from Philadelphia to my classes in Abington. I often nodded off during class. One time I got a speeding ticket while following a cop car up the highway.

"Have you been drinking?" he asked me.

"No, just getting off the night shift and heading to college," I said.

"Try sleeping at some point," the cop said while handing me the ticket. "And not on the highway. Pull over when you get tired."

My grade-point average fell from 3.7 to 1.7 in one term.

"What's going on with you?" my academic adviser, Bill Johnston, asked after grades came out. He had a good point. And I had a decision to make. Give up my $86 per week newspaper job, or drop out of college. I knew one or the other had to go. I just couldn't pull the trigger on quitting my first newspaper job. The ink was already getting into my blood.

One night, Dad called me into his bedroom.

"Son, I have to show you something," he said, reaching under his bed and pulling out a metal box. Inserting a key, he opened the box and pulled out some papers.

"If anything ever happens to me …"

"Nothing's going to happen to you, Dad," I immediately interjected. That old fear of death I had first noticed in 1961 after Dad's first heart attack came rushing back to me.

"I hope so," Dad said, "but if something does happen to me, these are my important papers," he said. "Your mother knows where they are, but you boys have to be strong for her."

Somehow, Dad had a premonition of his death. Maybe it was the angina pains he felt every day in his chest, or the nitroglycerin pills he took when the pain became too persistent. He had lived eight extra years after losing 50 percent of the muscle capacity in his heart following his first attack. We were lucky to have had him that long.

Dad died one Sunday morning – March 9, 1969 – while driving out of the steel mill following an 11-7 night shift in the Open Hearth. He had been showing around a newspaper clipping of me and Tim, who were featured the day before for having made the honor roll at Penn State back in the fall of 1968. Dad left work that morning, then realized he had forgot the clipping, climbed back up three flights of stairs to his locker, walked back out to the parking lot, and died not long after starting up his car.

Larry was also working the night shift. He saw Dad's car along the side of the road. It was empty. Larry soon learned that Dad had been taken to the company's emergency center. When he got there, Dad's brother Albert intercepted Larry and told him the bad news. Dad was dead.

Poor Larry, still only 18 years old, had to go home and tell his mother. But first he went and picked up his Aunt Clara, Mom's sister, and brought her with him to the house. Larry grew up all in one day, the hardest way imaginable.

The biggest funerals are always for the people who die young. Dad, at 53, was one of the first of his group of friends to pass away. Mourners packed the funeral home. A long line extended out the front door and into the parking lot. We shook hands with people for hours on end, hearing them tell us what a great guy Dad was.

"Your father treated me as kindly as anyone I ever met," said one of his co-workers, a black man with the unlikely nickname of "Ice Cream."

Dad's bowling team gave me a plaque at the league banquet in late April, inscribed with these simple words: "To A Great Competitor and Friend." One of the guys looked at me and said, "A team is nothing without its captain." And that was the end of it for me. I grabbed my jacket and plaque and headed home. Mom and I sat down on the living room couch. We cried into each other's arms, finally letting out all the grief we had internalized over the six weeks since Dad had died.

"The thing he wanted most of all during the year you were gone," Mom told me, "was to live long enough to see you come home from Vietnam."

It was now the spring of 1969. All the guys I knew in Vietnam had returned home safely. Rosey and I met for dinner and found we had little in common back home in the real world. (We would find much to talk about when we met again 34 years later.) Bill Kimball tried to call me one day. My Aunt Clara took the call and failed to get a return number. That would be my final contact with any of the guys until March of 2003, in Las Vegas.

CHAPTER NINE:
BURYING MY MILITARY PAST

RETURNING VETERANS STOOD APART FROM regular students on college campuses back in 1969. Many wore some part of their old uniforms, just to let people know they had served. It was a natural thing to do at the time. It just wasn't my style at all. I was trying to go to school undercover, incognito, sneaking around like the Viet Cong. Reluctant soldier makes the transition into college life.

I met a few veterans along the way, and found them patriotic about their service and disapproving of anyone who hadn't served. We got along because veterans trusted anyone who had been drafted or enlisted, especially someone who had been in Vietnam.

Here was my problem. I didn't feel good about my year in Vietnam. I wanted to place my two years in the Army on the back burner and get back to living life as a normal college student. I wanted to make up for my "lost years" that Uncle Sam had taken away from me.

Using this approach, I ended up stuck between two distinct campus cultures. Veterans, especially Vietnam veterans, were a visible minority looked upon with some disdain by student activists. So my technique was to bury my military past, bringing it up only in the company of other veterans, and only when necessary. Most students had no idea I was a veteran.

I managed to survive nearly two years at Penn State-Ogontz without having to deal with my own ambiguity about the war. And then Kent State happened in early May of 1970. Four college students were killed by nervous National Guard troopers called out to quell a protest on the central Ohio campus. Within days, campuses around the country were scenes of mass protests.

Few students had any interest in going to class. A number of activist professors at Ogontz chose to hold seminars instead of classes, inviting students to sit on the grass outside the classroom, breathing fresh air and opening minds to free discussion. Kids were getting stoned before the seminars. One day, we found out that all classroom grading would be done on a pass-fail system. There would be no As, Bs and Ds this semester. You either passed or failed! Only serious students took issue with this decision.

Bill Johnston saw me on the lawn one afternoon, sitting in the back, not contributing to the discussion, just minding my own business.

"What do you think of all this?" he asked, knowing from prior conversations that I was less than two years removed from Vietnam.

"I'm just looking at the girls," I replied. Bill was only 30 years old and had eyes like the rest of us. Young women never looked better than they did in the early 1970s.

"Seriously, what do you think about Kent State?"

"Hard to believe it could happen in this country," I said, "but if you get a bunch of nervous soldiers with guns and put them in the middle of a confrontation, I can see how it happened. They never should have let those National Guardsmen have bullets."

"How are you on the war?" Bill asked.

"I didn't know much about it when I got drafted," I said. "But any soldier who goes to war comes back a changed person. We're wrong to have gone in there, no question about it. There's just something about this country that we keep getting ourselves into these stupid wars overseas."

"We were isolationists before World War II," the young professor pointed out.

"Yeah, that's what I read in the history books," I said. "And now we're the self-appointed policeman for the world. That's a pretty tough job to take on."

Some students began singing protest songs after class ended, making it difficult to continue our conversation. It was pretty amazing to hear them sing from memory the words to songs like "Where Have All the Flowers Gone" and "Blowing in the Wind."

"I hope nothing bad happens to these kids," Johnston said. "They're beautiful."

He was right. These kids were the innocents. We veterans had lost that quality two or three years earlier, depending upon when we served in Vietnam. I think I went from 19 years young to an old 30 in terms of how I looked at life. I had seemingly lost the ability to laugh about silly stuff. I looked at people who were really happy and wondered how they could smile so much. Was it Vietnam that had changed me? Had my father's sudden death taken the joy out of my life? Or did I have that kind of somber personality all along?

I went through my college years feeling a separation from these slightly younger peers of mine. My first two years were spent as a commuting student to Ogontz, just 20 miles from home, and that made interacting with fellow students random at best. When I arrived at Penn State's main campus in the summer of 1970, and had to live on campus for the first semester, I started to make friends with regular students and get back into a normal college social life.

I got a job on the student newspaper's sports staff in the fall of 1970, covering the varsity men's soccer team, coached by Herb Schmidt, a former All-American who had served two years in the Army from 1965-67, reaching the rank of captain. Herb carried himself with a strong military bearing and expected his players to play the game with discipline. As his team depended upon several creative players from Philadelphia, Herb was also flexible enough to let their individual talents shine through.

It was interesting to see how Schmidt handled his team. Despite his military background, he looked the other way on long bus rides home from road games, knowing that some of his kids might be passing around a bottle to warm themselves up. When the bus reached campus, though, Herb would stand up and reassert his control with a stern speech and instructions about the next day's practice session.

Herb and I never talked about the Army. He saw sports writers as some kind of annoyance, a typical sentiment among coaches at all levels of sport. I saw him as a rigid reminder of a few serious officers I had served under in the Army. Herb was an authority figure, and the war had turned me off on people in charge. Not sure why.

For the last game of the football season, I got a promotion to football writer for the student newspaper and sat in the press box, watching Head Coach Joe Paterno's Nittany Lions finish off a disappointing 7-3 season with an easy win over Pittsburgh. Within a few weeks, I would be promoted to sports editor in place of the graduating Dan Donovan.

Suddenly I had a new direction in life, a new purpose. Having always loved sports, I was now in a position to write about the games, and not just about any old team. Penn State's programs were nationally prominent in football and wrestling. The basketball team lurked on the outer fringes of the Top 25 back when that meant something.

I moved into an apartment with two veterans who were just as happy to be finished with their service as I was. Joe Dunleavy had been an Army lieutenant who served in Germany. The easy-going Philadelphian drank beers and told funny stories while seemingly spending very little time worrying about his schoolwork.

Ex-Marine Rich Rivell, our other roomie, majored in computer science and spent many evenings at the computer lab, working up programs in a field that was going to change all of our lives over the next 40 years.

I asked Rich one night what drove him to work so hard.

"Writing computer programs is almost addictive," he said. "I get started with it and I can't stop. I just love it." Rich went on to a successful career in this burgeoning industry.

We were putting our military experiences behind us, the three of us, as the spring of 1971 came around. But the war was still raging. Nixon had sent troops into Cambodia the previous spring. My old A Battery was one of several units that crossed the border into Cambodia, something I never learned until 30 years later. And while our military presence in Vietnam was rapidly diminishing, we still had more than 150,000 troops in South Vietnam.

Anti-war protestors had much to rage about in 1971. As the one-year anniversary of the Kent State massacre approached, the peace movement decided to encourage marches against the war all across the country. Penn State, hardly the most radical of campuses, would be the scene of a small but vocal rally downtown, at the foot of the campus.

I managed to get mixed up in this over a few beers one night. Ed Baker, head of the Veterans Organization at Penn State, came into The Rathskeller and spotted me and my two roomies pounding down a few Rolling Rocks.

"Are you guys going to march against the protestors tomorrow?" he asked.

"What's going on?" Rich said.

"Well, a bunch of veterans are going to form up at the west end of College Avenue. We're going to help the cops stop this protest march."

"Ah, not for me," I told Baker. My roomies agreed this seemed like foolishness. Let the kids march. It's their war now. We were over it.

The next morning, I was sitting in a classroom, minding my own business, when an attractive co-ed came over, leaned close, and asked if

I would be marching against the war this afternoon. She didn't know me from Adam, but I had already taken the bait.

"Sure," I said. "Where are you meeting?"

"Just come with me after class ends," she said.

And that's how I got involved in my only anti-war protest march. A bunch of us "protestors" formed up at the east end of College Avenue, listened to instructions from a few ringleaders, and then walked into the street. I declined to hold a sign that mocked President Nixon. (Regret that now.) There were a couple hundred of us, many holding signs, some smoking dope, others, like me, just up for a good walk in the afternoon air.

We marched for several blocks, singing "Four Dead in Ohio" and chanting "1-2-3-4, What Are We Fighting For?" It was all good fun. But as we approached the South Allen Street intersection, police cars could be seen blinking at the red light two blocks ahead. It looked like this is where the march would end, and perhaps not in a peaceful manner. Ed Baker and some other veterans were lined up behind the police, holding signs of their own. "Hippies Go Home" and "Get a Job!" were the best they could come up with.

As we marched toward our meeting with the police, we passed one of my favorite bars, a French Bistro with tables and chairs located outside on the front sidewalk. I heard my name called.

"Terry! Over here! Have a beer!" Joe Dunleavy was sitting at a table with some of his veteran friends who would rather drink beer than march, either for or against the war. I joined them.

We watched from the bistro as protestors approached the police roadblock. If this were a radical campus, some heads would have been knocked, and signs busted by the cops. But this was Penn State, stuck in the middle of rural Pennsylvania. We had some radicals. Just not many of them. The police arrested an activist professor named Wells Keddie, along with a few student protestors. Most of the others just stood around and watched, then broke into small groups and headed back down

College Avenue. A fair amount of them invaded The Rathskeller to wash down their frustrations with a case or two of Rolling Rock.

Beer was a common bond among protestors and veterans in those days. Pot, too.

Later that summer, I would write an article for *The Daily Collegian* on Professor Keddie, who happened to live right next door to me in an apartment complex off campus.

Keddie revealed what his original dream in life had been.

"I wanted to be a sports writer when I was your age," he said, laughing at the idea.

"What happened?"

"Life happened," he said. "The person I was at 21 is not the person I am today, 30 years later. You change as you get older. You evolve. I evolved into a Labor Relations professor with some dark thoughts about America's foreign policy."

I was 24 by now and had changed a lot over the past five years. Vietnam had impacted my life, turned me from a sarcastic teenager into a cynical young adult. I carried some shame about my involvement in the war, even though I had been drafted and could always rationalize my forced participation in this dubious adventure.

The next day, the sweet co-ed from class stopped me outside Sackett Building, where our student newspaper staff toiled. She wanted to talk.

"Somebody told me you were a Vietnam veteran," she said as we sat down on the grass. "I never knew that."

"Well, it's not something I like to advertise."

"But you marched with the protestors?"

"Yes. I want the war over as much as anyone."

"Were you always against the war?"

"I was only 19 when I got drafted back in 1966," I said. "I was way too young to have formed an opinion on Vietnam."

"Very few people had," she said. "I was 15 and did not know what people were talking about when they said someone from our neighborhood had gone to Vietnam. It was just a word to me, the name of a country that didn't mean anything."

I nodded in agreement.

"And now look at us. Everyone knows where Vietnam is. Over 50,000 Americans have died in Vietnam."

"Are you sorry you went?" she asked me.

"Not really," I said. "Believe it or not, I met some great people over there. I learned first-hand what war was like, and fortunately I was in a fairly safe place where death wasn't something you thought about every day."

I still didn't know her name. Classes at Penn State featured as many as 140 students. It was like a small city in the big auditorium where we had met.

"What's your name?" I asked. "You seem like someone I should know."

"You don't know my name?" she asked. "I'm insulted! I know yours! … I'm Bonnie. I grew up in Meadville. My dad fought in World War II. If he knew I was marching against the war, he'd drive up here and pull me off campus … What do your parents think about the war?"

"My dad died in 1969," I said. "He had mixed feelings about the war by the time I got home. I think a lot of his friends did, too. This war reminds older people so much of Korea. When you see kids from your hometown coming home in boxes from Vietnam, well, that starts to add up. Nixon is losing his 'Silent Majority.' He'll be lucky to get re-elected next year." (Not true. He won in a landslide over peace candidate George McGovern, a decorated World War II veteran.)

Bonnie and I became fast friends over that summer of 1971. The relationship lasted until early autumn, when she became interested in a fellow peace activist. The one thing she did was get me talking about Vietnam again, giving me a chance to "evolve," as Wells Keddie liked to say.

I finished my undergraduate days at Penn State in the spring of 1972. Tim and I graduated at the same time (Larry would earn a degree in landscape architecture from PSU in 1975). Mom came up for the ceremony and we took her out to dinner. Our father was an unspoken presence, someone we thought about whenever we were together. He would have loved to visit Penn State on a football weekend and experience all the fun. Dad's time had come, too, and we knew we were fortunate to have him for eight years after his first heart attack.

The war dragged on in Vietnam through 1974. Nixon reduced our commitment of troops until we were back to the adviser levels of the early 1960s. Our soldiers were just targets by this point, ordered to keep away from battles, as the Viet Cong took control of the countryside and the North Vietnamese Army moved freely into the upper half of South Vietnam. The South Vietnamese Army had no stomach for fighting, as always.

My issues with Vietnam were becoming more distant. The only residual problem I had occurred late at night when I was driving home from work. For some reason, I visualized people shooting at me from cars on the other side of the road. That went on for a few months and then went away, never to return.

The Paris Peace Talks continued, taking small steps towards peace. But the United States just wouldn't give in, so it took a final offensive by the VC and NVA in 1975 to chase our personnel out of the U.S. Embassy in Saigon. We all watched on television as soldiers and embassy officials left by chopper from the roof of the building while the Viet Cong and NVA pressed their attack outside the embassy gates.

Our country had never witnessed such a humiliating defeat. It was April 30, 1975, a date the nation quickly forgot. And what did we feel as citizens when the war ended? Veterans felt no different than the protestors.

"What a waste," we all believed. I remember feeling a little alone the night Saigon fell, drinking beers in downtown State College with friends who weren't veterans. Vietnam was just another news story to them, a reminder, perhaps, of a tight squeeze in their lives back in the late 1960s when the draft still loomed over the heads of teenage males. The draft had been eliminated in 1973 and now the war was over. The protestors had nothing to protest anymore, except Watergate and Dick Nixon.

After graduating in March of 1972, I took a job at State College's morning newspaper, an irreverent publication called *The Pennsylvania Mirror*. It was fitting that I replaced a sports editor named Bill Greene, whose hair had turned white during his year in Vietnam. Bill had been an infantryman who saw a lot of action early in the war, back in 1965. He was heading to South Carolina to take a sports editor's job, creating an opportunity for me to continue reporting on Penn State's sports teams, and the high school programs in surrounding towns.

Bill and I had a similar take on football after spending time in a real war.

"You hear all these analogies to war after football games," Bill told me one day right before he left town. "Some coaches and players compare football to war. I can't honestly write that. Not anymore."

Midway through my seven years covering Penn State football, Joe Paterno brushed off some rare criticism by pointing out that sports writers had never played the game and therefore couldn't comment accurately, or make criticisms, on what they had just witnessed.

Joe paraphrased a speech Teddy Roosevelt made nearly 60 years before, the famous "Man in the Arena" speech that honored the person who fights the fight, not the critic who reports the news.

I had to look up Teddy's speech to fully understand what Paterno was talking about:

"It is not the critic who counts, not the man who points out how the strong man stumbled, or where the doer of deeds could have done them better. The credit belongs to the man who is actually in the arena, whose face is marred by dust and sweat and blood; who strives valiantly; who errs and comes short again and again; who knows the great enthusiasms, the great devotions, and spends himself in a worthy cause; who, at best, knows

in the end the triumph of high achievement; and who, at the worst, if he fails, at least fails while daring greatly, so this place shall never be with those cold and timid souls who know neither victory or defeat."

Even though Joe was putting his sports writer critics down through the powerful words of a great man, I felt good, because I realized that I had been in an arena, too, and lived to tell the tale. It was another small step for me in coming to grips with my service in Vietnam.

Vietnam impacted so many lives from my generation, whether you served in the military or burned your draft card. I would happen upon veterans in the strangest places. One time, I wrote a story for The Collegian about a fraternity's intramural rugby team and its star player, a long-haired, bearded fellow named Nazar Bambazoody.

"That's not your real name, is it?" I asked him, half in jest. Nazar just smiled and said nothing. A few years later, I learned that he was an Army deserter who drifted back to his old college fraternity and took a job as cook, waiting out the war in familiar surroundings.

I would remain in State College until November of 1977, working hard and playing even harder, finally running myself into a career dead end. I partied frequently in my final few years in town, a not uncommon occurrence in a college town loaded with bars and young people. Sometimes my drinking mixed with my job, never a good thing. I was beginning to fall short of the standards I had set for myself. Still, if I drank too much, it wasn't because I went to Vietnam. It was more about just having too much fun in a college town. If I failed to sustain any relationships with women, it was because my job made me work the night shift too often. I was in denial about my drinking and an inability to go deep into friendships.

My newspaper, never a financial success during its nine years of existence, ceased publication on Dec. 31, 1977. I was 30 years old by then and ready to move on from the cozy, sheltered life of a college town.

CHAPTER TEN:
OUT IN THE REAL WORLD

I SETTLED INTO A SPORTS EDITOR'S job in Doylestown, Pa., 20 miles north of my hometown, in the summer of 1978. My new boss was a veteran newspaperman from Philadelphia named Jim McFadden, who ran his newsroom with a hard heart and an iron fist. McFadden liked the way I handled myself in an interview for a sports writing position and made me editor of his three-man sports department on the spot. And things were good for a while at *The Intelligencer* in Doylestown.

One day, I met a Vietnam veteran named Mike Bass, who limped into the office and introduced himself to me.

"How did you hurt your leg?" I asked him. Mike was wearing army pants and boots so I had an inkling of what might be coming.

"I was a machine gunner on a gunship in 'Nam," he began. "Got myself shot in the leg. We were going out on a 'milk run' one day. That's a mission where you don't expect any contact. Our other gunner didn't want to make the trip. Some career sergeant who worked behind a desk asked if he could man that gun. He could get another ribbon for his chest if he flew a combat mission. I didn't think it would be a problem. The guy seemed to know what he was doing.

"Well, we got up into the air and wouldn't you know it, we ran into heavy contact. A company of VC had a couple platoons of our infantry pinned down. We were the only gunship in the area and we started to lay down some fire. Then I noticed the sergeant. He was frozen over his gun. Couldn't even pull the trigger. I alerted our pilot and he began sweeping down over the VC using only my side of the chopper. Later on, we got a report that 30 VC were killed, most of them from my gun.

"The infantry guys down on the ground were actually cheering as we passed by on each run. My gun was really smoking that day."

"So how did your knee get messed up?"

"You wouldn't believe it," Mike said. "When the VC pulled out, we noticed one wounded Charlie down on the ground. My pilot wanted to go down and take him as a POW. I told him it was okay. All the shooting seemed to have stopped. Infantry had secured the area, or so we thought. We landed and I ran out to check on this gook. When I got there, they opened up on me from the woods and I caught one in the back of my left knee. Almost a million dollar wound. I thought I was going home, but they had me back in action within a month."

I was amazed by this story.

"Wait a minute," I said. "You killed 30 VC and then you went back to take one as a POW?"

"Right." Mike looked kind of sheepish about the whole story. "The war seems like a long time ago for me," he added, "except I have this reminder in my left leg that won't let me forget."

This was the first time I had lived near home in eight years. Many of my old friends were back in the area, pursuing their careers and chasing some fun in their down time. Life revolved around work, golf, softball, bowling leagues, water skiing at the lake and drinking beer at our local pub, Puss 'N Boots. My brother Larry had married his college sweetheart, Tricia Scanlan, and formed his own landscaping company. Tim went back to school and became a guidance counselor, eventually working for 35 years at a New Jersey high school. Oldest brother Dan, who had acquired his father's love of travel, remained on the West Coast after getting out of the Army and was now teaching at a community college in British Columbia. He would meet his future wife Elaine McGee there, and eventually they would return to the East Coast, finally settling in Nova Scotia.

At least half the guys in our crowd were veterans. Some had gone to Vietnam. None of them talked about it much. Dave Livingston went into the Marines and never spoke about what he had seen in Vietnam. Dave was an easygoing guy on all other subjects, but he clammed up about the war and I never pushed him on it. I think it was Dave's silence that told me so much about my own experience in Vietnam. I was one of the fortunate ones who got away pretty clean from the war.

"There's a big difference between infantry and artillery," I told Larry one night when he asked me about Vietnam. "Infantry go out in the jungle and chase the enemy. Heavy artillery units, like the one I was in, operated in fire support bases and usually had protection on their perimeter. I couldn't imagine the guts it would take to go out into the jungle at night."

Two high school buddies who grew up in my neighborhood were killed in Vietnam. Eddie Beers, whom we would often see at the local Methodist Church, went into the Marines and was killed in 1968. Ricky Guest, who lived one street over from us, died in a Jeep accident in Vietnam. His was ruled a "non-combat" death, which was a form of distinction I could never understand. You're riding a Jeep down a muddy road in a war zone, on the side of a hill, and it flips over, killing two or three soldiers. How is that not a combat death?

Hollywood started to crank out movies about Vietnam in the late 1970s. *Apocalypse Now* was the best of the early flicks. It was a little deep and creepy as Martin Sheen chased Marlon Brando off into Cambodia to execute the insane Colonel "with extreme malice."

The Deerhunter, featuring Robert DeNiro, Meryl Streep, and Christopher Walken, included some laughable hunting scenes. DeNiro didn't even know how to hold his rifle, not surprising for a guy who grew up in New York City. Walken's character found a Russian roulette game in Saigon to spice up the movie. Never met a Vietnam veteran who heard of such a thing. Of course, most of us didn't spend any sustained time in Saigon, not with a war going on out in the bush.

Vietnam vets were portrayed in the movies, and often in real life, as dangerous people. If a Vietnam vet went crazy one day and shot up his workplace, the newspaper headlines usually focused on his military background. And since drug use had become so common among soldiers during the final five years of the war, this became a stereotype, too. Drug-addled Vietnam veteran runs amuck in shopping mall!

The post-World War II media treatment of veterans was much kinder, even though that war ruined more than its fair share of lives. Hollywood took a patriotic stance prior to, during, and after the big war ended. *"Best Years of Our Lives"* won an Oscar in 1947 for its story of three soldiers who came home together and tried to fit back into their community. It was an honest portrayal of soldiers coming home from war and it ended on a positive note. There was nothing uplifting about 1976's *Apocalypse Now*, except perhaps for Robert Duvall's great line about napalm: "It smells like ... victory!" As moviegoers, we all loved that one. The harsh reality of flaming gasoline scorching Vietnamese soldiers and civilians was another story altogether.

If napalm smelled like victory, the Iranian Hostage Crisis went to the other end of our national self-esteem. Fifty-two American diplomats and workers at our Embassy in Tehran were taken hostage on Nov. 4, 1979 and held for the next 444 days as the world watched. Americans had barely escaped from our embassy in Saigon in 1975 and now we couldn't protect our workers in Iran just four years later. We watched helplessly as the Iranian militants paraded their hostages in front of television cameras. America reached rock-bottom when eight servicemen died in a failed attempt to rescue the hostages on April 24, 1980.

It had only been 35 years since the United States helped save the world from Adolph Hitler and Japanese imperialism. Now, after a failed intervention in Vietnam and a revolution in Iran that shed the last shackles of colonialism in that country, America's military prowess and prestige were at an all-time low. That feeling pervaded every-day life. Scenes of the hostages in chains made the news every night. They finally gained their freedom when Ronald Reagan took office on Jan. 20, 1981.

If you were a veteran, this was not a good time to feel like a proud American. I just shoved my own service deeper into a hole, reminded of it only while reading a book about Vietnam, or when Hollywood gave us another movie on the subject. And even that was risky business for the film makers because Vietnam movies did not sell many tickets in 1981. We were a country depressed about war and our frequent incursions into other countries.

Soldiers have a quick way to deal with bad news. They just say "fuck it" and move on. That bad attitude was invading my professional life. My anti-authority syndrome, first developed in the Army, now appeared in my professional career. I decided to take on my boss, who often resembled one of those tyrannical officers you see in bad movies. McFadden, spittle flying from the corners of his lips, would come raging into the office some mornings, begin tearing apart pages in the production room, and berate offending editors or reporters for the mistakes he perceived they had made.

One day, this often-angry editor blistered a young reporter in the middle of the newsroom, screaming at her for failing to put a politician's middle initial into a story. It was a scene out of the *Caine Mutiny*, with McFadden playing Bogart's role, seemingly ready to measure how much strawberry ice cream was missing.

"We always run middle initials of elected officials in this newspaper!" he shouted. The woman began tearing up under the duress. I wouldn't take it any longer.

"Boss," I said, rising to my feet. "Can't you at least criticize people in your office, instead of the middle of the newsroom?"

He looked at me with scorn. Our honeymoon was over. And within six months, I would be looking for a new job, eventually moving to Rhode Island and staying there for the rest of my life.

CHAPTER ELEVEN: "THE WALL" HEALS VIETNAM VETS

"THE WALL" IS WHERE THE healing process began for me, and a lot of other Vietnam veterans, too.

Known officially as the Vietnam Veterans Memorial, initial construction of The Wall was completed in Washington, D.C.'s Constitution Gardens in November of 1982. It immediately attracted throngs of Vietnam veterans, many of whom were searching for a place to lay down their own emotional wounds. The Wall became our version of the Welcome Home parade we never got, nor expected, from a war that wasn't over when we came home.

Still, it took me two years to get down to Washington.

Once you settle down into the rhythm of life, the years seem to roll by effortlessly. That's how it appeared to me after I moved to Rhode Island in 1982, locked myself into a decent job, and met the woman who would challenge me for the rest of my life. I never thought I would stay more than five years in Rhode Island but here I am, 31 years later, retired and looking back, wondering where all the years have gone.

After leaving my previous job abruptly, I wanted to establish some stability and stay a few years in Pawtucket, working as sports editor of the *Evening Times*. It took me two years to find this job. In the interim, I worked for Larry's landscaping company, raking leaves and weeding gardens. This was a humbling kind of work that taught me a few lessons I would take into my next job. No more taking on the boss for me! My old high school pal Joe Hodgson hired me on as a construction site laborer. I almost got myself electrocuted on that job, eating 220 volts while ripping out some wires from the ceiling. I was in over my head in the demolition business and needed to get back to the safety of newspapers real soon. The Pawtucket job came just in time.

Vietnam was now just a distant memory. Our country had forgotten this dark chapter in its history, too, moving into the era of Ronald Reagan, a likeable old Hollywood actor most Baby Boomers remembered as the TV host of "Death Valley Days" back in 1964-65.

Our military took another major hit on Oct. 23, 1983 when terrorists exploded two truck bombs at a multinational military barracks in Beirut, Lebanon, killing 241 U.S. troops, including 220 Marines. It was the largest single-day death toll for the Marines since the battle for Iwo Jima near the end of World War II. Two days later, in an unrelated move, the U.S. invaded Grenada, a tiny Caribbean Island, ostensibly to free some American medical students held hostage by the local militia.

The mission was completed in three weeks, amid cries of American imperialism from, among others, Great Britain and Canada. The United Nations called the invasion a "flagrant violation of international law." Even our allies didn't like us anymore.

It was, however, a victory for the American military, its first since World War II. Although we once again had stuck our nose where it didn't belong, Americans could at least feel good about the final outcome, which was freedom for the medical students and a deposed military dictatorship in Grenada.

I visited the Vietnam Veterans Memorial for the first time in 1984, at the urging of my girlfriend, Cheryl Britland. In the year we had known each other, Cheryl and I had already done some traveling, and after we visited Valley Forge earlier in 1984 and then saw where Washington crossed the Delaware (only 10 miles from where I grew up), we knew we had to go to the nation's capital and see "The Wall."

My interest in military history had been gradually developing over the past decade. In addition, Cheryl's father was a World War II veteran who attended reunions of his old Army Air Corps unit every year. Bill Britland was the first World War II veteran I ever talked to at length and he would be a source of inspiration over the next 20 years as I sought to find my own meaning to the word "veteran." Bill took so much pride in being a veteran that I think it started to rub off on me.

"The Wall" became a place people visited to pay their respects to the more than 58,000 soldiers who lost their lives in Vietnam. The site itself evoked eerie memories for veterans. It consisted of two long, black walls nearly 250 feet long, sunk into the ground, tapering from a height of 10 feet in the middle to eight inches at the far corners. They are shaped in the form of the letter V. Names of all the dead soldiers are engraved in the black-cut stone.

One side of the wall points in the direction of the Washington Monument. The other points towards the Lincoln Memorial. Conceived by a then 22-year-old college student named Maya Lin, The Wall is made of reflective stone. When a visitor looks closely, he sees the names of dead soldiers, along with a reflection of himself. It is pretty spooky stuff, especially in the fading twilight hours.

We arrived in late afternoon and spent several hours walking up and down Constitution Gardens. We stopped at the directory to look up three names: Kevin Dugan, Eddie Beers and Rick Guest. Seeing Dugan's name on the shiny stone panel created an immediate sense of sadness for me, sadness over the life he never got to live out fully. This was true for all of the names on The Wall, of course, but Dugan was one I had served with. I knew he had dreams, too, and his would never be fulfilled.

Everyone walking through the monument area seemed lost in their own thoughts. We were former soldiers, brothers, sisters, children, mothers and fathers, or just friends of servicemen who had died in Vietnam. People with no attachments to Vietnam came to see what this haunting memorial stood for. And it didn't take long for The Wall to become one of the most popular monuments in the nation's capital.

This was my first trip to D.C. since 1966, when I passed through on a troop train that stopped briefly at Union Station to collect soldiers from the D.C. area. It is, of course, the city of our national government, and all of those wonderful monuments. The Vietnam Veterans Memorial Wall certainly found its place among the great tributes to our soldiers. In fact, it came into existence years ahead of similar projects dedicated to soldiers of World War II and the Korean War.

Cheryl and I would tour many military battlegrounds over the next two decades, from Antietam in Maryland to Chattanooga in Tennessee and even Little Big Horn up in Montana, where Custer made his last stand. All of those sites have a special reverence about them, a haunting feeling of death and destruction that transports you back in time, back to when the battles were fought so many years before. While touring the country with Cheryl, my love for America, and for her, crystallized at the same time. We were both filled with adrenalin when we jumped in our car and drove from New England to the Deep South, or took a plane to Arizona and rented a car, riding through Tombstone and visualizing the world that Wyatt Earp lived in barely 100 years earlier. It was dawning on me that this really is a great country we live in, a place worth fighting for. My country, right or wrong? Probably.

At Gettysburg, we looked for the name of my mother's great-grandfather, Isaac Kenvin, who served in the Pennsylvania's 81st Infantry unit as a bugle boy. We walked around and around the Pennsylvania Monument, looking over the long lists of names engraved on various mounted plaques, until we found the one we were looking for. I had never really been truly appreciative of my veteran status until the moment I spied Isaac Kenvin's name on the monument. But now I could see a family link between 1863 and 1967. Isaac probably had a few ugly stories to tell about his service in the Civil War! He might have even been drafted.

My reading habits changed from sports and entertainment biographies to military history as the 1980s turned into the 1990s. I read about Patton, Eisenhower, Teddy Roosevelt and many others who fought for our country. Went back and re-read Norman Mailer's *"The Naked and the Dead,"* and Herman Wouk's *"The Caine Mutiny."* I tore through a few Vietnam books. By the late 1990s, Michael Herr's *"Dispatches"* and John Laurence's *"The Cat from Hue"* came along to fit my feelings about the war. They were both journalists who brought their natural cynicism with them to Vietnam. They also brought their sense of humor, without which we would all be in big trouble in a war zone.

Mailer's book depicted the brutality of war like few others ever have. When you read biographies of heroes like Patton and Ike and Teddy Roosevelt, war is painted as this ultimate test of courage and perseverance. Generals are proud leaders torn by the anguish involved in sending men to their deaths. Infantryman are just cannon fodder. Their lives are traded during battles that often have no meaning. Mailer's book focused on the foot soldier trying to fight his way out of the jungle during World War II. He was 25 when he finished it and had served as a cook during the war. Amazing.

In 1991, America returned to the battlefield when Iraq's Saddam Hussein invaded one of our oil-producing allies, Kuwait. And here we saw war glamorized as never before, war on television, live, with breathless correspondents talking over video coverage as our bombs slammed into the heart of Bagdad. The war only lasted a few weeks, but it became a nightly staple for television viewers. Iraqi soldiers and civilians were dying under all those bombs, something we knew deep down and refused to admit because it was just exciting television to see our new high-tech weapons in action.

Enhanced by computer technology, artillery accuracy had changed greatly since Vietnam. Where we used to "bracket" targets in the old days, firing an initial round and then adjusting elevation and/or on the next round, Gulf War technology gave us the "smart bomb" that could go around corners of buildings and hit its target on the first attempt. I was fascinated by this development. What was wrong with me? The kid who came to realize we had no business in Vietnam now was a middle-aged man getting his kicks watching our modern weapons demolish buildings in Bagdad. I even felt a little sad when the fighting stopped and we no longer could watch CNN's coverage on television every night. And I wasn't alone, of course. TV ratings all around the country showed that Americans were fascinated by the First Gulf War.

We would become a nation deeply involved in war, again, over the next 20 years sending our troops to Somalia, Bosnia, back to Iraq and into Afghanistan after terrorists killed nearly 3,000 Americans on our own soil on Sept. 11, 2001. This was the darkest day in American history since Pearl Harbor nearly 60 years earlier. We finally had a real reason to fight again, and young people flocked to enlist in our Armed Services, which had become an all-volunteer organization over the past 30 years.

Like most Americans, I had no reservations about chasing Osama bin Laden into Afghanistan right away, as President George W. Bush indicated he would do. It got a little more complicated with Iraq as our leaders debated the existence of "weapons of mass destruction" inside that country. But, like most Americans, I backed the President, making the same mistake we made as a country back in the early 1960s when Vietnam appeared on our war plate. It was almost "our country, right or wrong," all over again. Patriotism is a dangerous emotion that cuts both ways.

In the run-up to Gulf War II, I had connected again with my old Army buddies from Vietnam. I found Bill Kimball on the "Proud Americans" website set up for 2/32 Artillery members by a fellow Vietnam Veteran, Chuck Healey. Pooling our resources, Kimball and I managed to locate seven other members of our FDC section – Chuck Rosenblum, Carl Miller, Tom Barrett, Ken Barbian and Bill Grelecki, along with two officers, Norm Gunderson and Tony Hoehner.

We decided to have a reunion in Las Vegas in late March of 2003, just in time for the start of the second Iraq War. And on a Friday afternoon, I made my way to the Treasure Island hotel lobby, where we planned to convene for drinks. Did we change much? Turns out we were all older and fatter and grayer but essentially the same people we knew from so long ago.

Adding irony to the affair, our ambitious Uncle Sam (a world-class cop) arranged another war in a far-off place that we could monitor on television during our visit. And we had the added enjoyment of seeing anti-war demonstrators show up in the streets of America, protesting the Bush family's latest incursion into Iraq. It seemed just like old times.

We had all served with "A" battery of the 2nd Battalion, 32nd Artillery unit between 1967 and 1969. There was no heavy lifting of projectiles for this crew. Most of us toiled in the Fire Direction Center, plotting targets on maps, computing firing data and relaying that information to the gun crews.

"We were all part of a team that worked hard to accomplish our objectives," Kimball, still a Chicago police officer, said. "If the Olympics had an event for firing artillery guns, we would have won the gold medal, hands down."

THIRD REUNION – In 2009, this group of 2/32 veterans gathered in Las Vegas. Left to right, front row: Jon Ringer, Chuck Rosenblum, Mike Neisius and his partner Carol Heffernan. Back row: Tony Hoehner, Carl Miller, Terry Nau, Dennis Wolfgang and son, Peg and Bill Kimball.

We had stories to tell all over again, mainly because we never got to try them out on one another once we returned stateside. Kimball and I couldn't wait to see the interaction between Norm Gunderson and Ken Barbian, who were involved in a brief altercation in Vietnam.

Kimball recalled the incident, straining his memory to get the basic facts right.

"Norm was a First Lieutenant who was well-liked and actually acted more like one of us 'draftees' than an officer," Kimball told me in 2012 as I prepared this book. "Norm used to walk around camp practicing karate moves on imaginary enemies. One day, Barbian, a young soldier from rural Texas with shoulders about three feet wide and strong as a bull, saw Gunderson practicing his moves and asked him what he was doing.

"Proud to explain, Gunderson told Barbian he was practicing karate, a self-defense martial art that he professed to be very good at. Barbian told Gunderson that if he ever tried using some of that stuff on him, he would be looking up at him from the ground. As I recall, Gunderson chuckled and said 'we will see' as he walked away.

"Several days later, Gunderson approached Barbian and tried to surprise him with a karate move. Before he even got close, Barbian hit Gunderson with a punch to the head that was more like a kick from a mule, and down he went. Gunderson shook it off, got up off the ground and walked away without saying a word. Nothing more ever came of the incident and we never saw Gunderson practicing karate again."

At the 2003 reunion, Gunderson had listened to Kimball and Barbian re-tell the story, smiled and bought a round of drinks. He was gracious and kind, still the leader of this aging group of veterans.

One of our FDC members had completed three years of college at Marquette University.

"The Army made me a cook," Bill Grelecki recalled with a laugh. "I only got switched to FDC after I came to Vietnam. Guess they had too many cooks and not enough FDC guys. Actually, I'm glad I learned how to cook in the Army. You never know when you're going to have to make a meal for a couple hundred people."

Carl Miller talked about his career cutting hair and supervising operations in his two barber shops back home in Indiana.

"I got my barber's license in 1965, even before I got drafted," Miller said. "I started out in Munster and finished there 40 years later. The last 15 years, I owned my own place with five chairs. I also started a Barber/Beauty Shop in nearby Highland. I never worked there, but owned it for 10 years. The business started changing. Some of my customers wanted a woman to cut their hair so I bought a shop close to mine, put all women in it, and every time a guy would say he wanted a female barber, I sent him to my other shop.

"Wait 'til they get women on the front lines," Miller said. "That should be interesting!"

Carl's wish came true in early 2013 when the Department of Defense gave an order to allow women into full combat situations.

There were stories told of mortar attacks and the panic they created. We recalled the death of Kevin Dugan, who became supply sergeant and drove his truck over a land mine while taking our laundry back to Tay Ninh base camp in September of 1968. Our zany battery clerk blew a hand off testing a bazooka-like weapon called "the Law" during the daily "Mad Minute."

The original stereotype of Vietnam veterans pictured them as dazed by war and crazed by their inability to cope when they came home, which certainly was true for a small percentage of veterans who saw worse things than we did.

For our group, there seemed to be just the normal rude awakenings in life to deal with. Two of us saw our fathers die suddenly after we got home, almost as if they hung on until we returned. Everyone seemed to have found successful careers and women to look after them. Most had children who were grown up by now.

Our reunion brought together middle-aged men who made the adjustment back into the real world and looked forward to the opportunity to talk about the one year in their lives when the adrenalin flowed as never before.

Gunderson, a West Point graduate, seemed more sentimental than the rest of us.

"After 35 years, we have our health," he said, holding up his glass for a toast prior to dinner. "And while, during the years, each of us might have endured some frustrations and setbacks, life has generally been kind. Of course, we know that others have not been so fortunate."

Gunderson, who would die in 2010, noted that seven of our nine reunion members were draftees.

"I think you should all feel proud that you answered when you were called and served your country well during some trying times."

And with the current Gulf War exploding across our television screens, Gunderson couldn't help but note the many divided sentiments that have once again begun to split our country.

"You continued to serve your country," he said, "by providing moral support to those who followed you. None of you has left the evaluation of the wisdom or justness of our wars, then and now, strictly to historians and politicians. This continuing debate and involvement that we see today is the very core of our democracy."

Most of us, it turned out, were in favor of the current war. And all of us wish it had never come to this point.

"I can't get September 11 out of my mind," Carl Miller said. "That's why we're fighting this war. We can't let dangerous people from around the world do something like that to us again."

Even though we spent most of the weekend eating and drinking and gambling, we did find time to watch a little bit of the emerging war.

Two days later, the first American POWs were pictured on television, looking scared and shaken, very similar to the way POWs had appeared when the North Vietnamese allowed them to be photographed during our war.

Suddenly this new war had become more than another faceless battle for all of us. A familiar knot settled in our stomachs as we remembered the cost of war. There is no such thing as a good war. People get wounded, captured and killed so often you almost become inured to the loss of human life.

"Let's hope it ends quickly," Gunderson said, and we all nodded our heads, praying that Iraq wouldn't become the "quagmire" we had all left behind a long time ago. (It took until 2011 to get most of our troops out of that crazy country.)

When our reunion ended, we had each come to learn the answer to that great unanswered question from the Vietnam War: Whatever happened to the guys we served with? Now we knew. We had become financial consultants, detectives, barbers, sports writers, tool-and-die shop owners, school teachers and salesmen.

That door we had closed upon coming home 35 years ago had been opened again in the most unlikely of places – Las Vegas. We vowed to meet again in a year or two, hopefully with a few more of our old friends in tow.

CHAPTER TWELVE: CONNECTING WITH OLDER VETERANS

HEADING INTO THE SEVENTH DECADE of my life, and my final few years in the newspaper business, I found myself looking at the people in our local sports world a little more closely, especially the older folks who had stories to tell of long careers and lives working around young people.

Early in March of 2008, as a new baseball season began to stir in Florida, I visited the owner of our local minor league baseball team in Pawtucket, a genial Frenchman from Woonsocket named Ben Mondor. Ben was 82 years old and something of a living legend throughout New England. He had saved the Pawtucket Red Sox from bankruptcy when he bought the team in 1976 and built it into one of the most successful franchises in minor league baseball.

I went to see Ben, figuring we would talk about baseball, and growing older, and anything else that popped into his agile mind. What I didn't expect was the story Ben would tell me about serving his adopted country during World War II.

"I graduated high school from Mount St. Charles Academy in 1942," Ben began. "They moved our graduation up a month because so many of us were heading into the military. That was an interesting time in my life. I got a letter from the government saying I had been drafted. But when I went to sign up, they told me I couldn't because I wasn't a citizen. I had been born in Quebec Province. My parents immigrated when I was a baby but we were so poor, and it was the Depression. Most of us immigrants never became citizens. That's still true today. It takes a long time.

"The government gave me a choice ... either enter the military or get deported at their expense to anywhere in the British Empire. Well, I went into the Navy. I was good at mathematics so they put me in navigation school. I ended up being assigned to the USS Whitworth. We boarded ship in California. The ship's captain was 27 years old. He said to me, 'Hey, Frenchman, get me to Hawaii.' I said it was due west and off we went. That was the beginning of my education in life. Our ship was assigned to the Pacific. Torpedo attacks were just something we lived with. The worst thing was the kamikaze attacks the Japanese started to use in 1944.

"The war made a man out of me. I learned some lessons that you can't find in college classes. Our ship was present in Tokyo Bay for the signing of the proclamation ending the war. Then we sailed off to dump our ship in a place called Green Cove, Florida.

"After that, some of us guys from New England were sent to Fargo Barracks in Boston for discharge from the Navy. Soon there were only nine of 10 of us left. I was wondering why I hadn't been discharged yet. Nobody would tell me. A couple more weeks went by and then an officer was kind enough to finally tell me the truth. 'You can't be discharged because you are in the Navy illegally, as an alien.' ... I spent three months at those Fargo Barracks. To get out of the Navy, I had to sign papers that basically waived me of my rights to the G.I. Bill and some health benefits I had coming.

"That made me bitter," Mondor said, the memory still fresh to this day. "Why me? I served in the Navy for four years. Was that illegal, all the things I accomplished as the ship's navigator?"

Mondor came home to Woonsocket, knowing only that he had to find a job and somehow get an education, even if he had been denied the G.I. Bill.

"I had to go to work," he said. "I did any kind of work I could find … sweeping floors, washing dishes, errand boy, working in the mills. I had to work to raise money for the business courses I ended up taking at Brown, the University of Rhode Island and any other school that would let me in.

"We were all hard workers in those days. That's the way we were raised during The Depression. You worked for everything you got. I finally got a steady job. All the while, I continued to try to get my citizenship. I went to classes with people who were just coming into the country.

"Years passed," Mondor said. "I finally got a letter from the government. It said to go to the Woonsocket courthouse at a certain day and time. Nothing else. I went there on the appointed day and was told to go to Room 23. I went there and a man comes in, shakes my hand. He's a judge. He tells me he is here to apologize on behalf of the United States government for its treatment of me. It was all a big paperwork blunder. He told me it was a pleasure to award me my citizenship after all these years."

The war had been over for 12 years.

"The thing I resented the most was losing my G.I. Bill rights," Ben said. "I could have gone to college for free, like all the other veterans. It just wasn't fair, what I had to go through.

FATHER FIGURE – Pawtucket Red Sox owner Ben Mondor, a World War II veteran, counseled many future big league baseball players, including Nomar Garciaparra. (Photo courtesy of Pawtucket Red Sox)

"I would consider the PawSox my life's legacy," Mondor concluded. "I've closed the door on my past, all the bitterness of my youth, the bitterness of losing my G.I. Bill after serving in the Navy for four years during the war. That is gone now ... although I do still have some resentment when I think about it.

"When I was inducted into the Boston Red Sox Hall of Fame a couple years ago," Mondor said, "I got back in my car and cried on the way home. Here was this little French kid from Woonsocket who was laughed at because he couldn't speak English. I said this is for all the people who laughed at me or held me back."

Ben's story bowled me over. When it was published the next day, he called on the phone and thanked me for writing about his youth.

"You never forget the person you were as a young man," he told me. I was on my own journey at the time, looking for that red-haired teenager who got drafted and headed off to war. Ben Mondor had given me a glimpse into how he handled his bitterness over being treated badly by the U.S. government. He was bitter, but he countered that negative emotion by going to work, pushing himself as hard as he could until he became a success in the business world, and then bought a baseball team that he would make his life's legacy.

A lot of us Vietnam veterans came home from the war with a bitter taste in our mouths. We didn't go off to fight a world-wide menace named Hitler the way Ben Mondor and his generation did. Our war was something else, something we couldn't quite define yet. It was more like Korea than World War II, and Korean veterans had come home to disappointment, too, realizing so many of their fellow soldiers had died for ... what?

Searching for answers, I did what any good newspaperman would do. I went out and started talking to people, interviewing veterans, listening more closely to my friends who had served in Korea and Vietnam, and seeking out younger veterans of the wars in Iraq and Afghanistan.

One of the more telling comments came from a Korean War veteran named Maurice Trottier.

"This was two or three years after I came home from Korea," Trottier told me one day in 2011. "I went into the 1271 Post on Hunt Street. The guy next to me asks, 'What war were you in?' And I said Korea. The guy looked at me and said he was in 'The Big War.' And that was the end of that conversation."

Trottier did find some meaning in the Korean War, although it took many years to come to this conclusion.

"You look at (South) Korea now and it makes you feel good," he said. "I think we did a good thing by going to war for the South Koreans."

Vietnam vets might say the same thing about their own war. The Socialist Republic of Vietnam has turned into a free-market economy, one of the fastest-growing economies in the world.

The war had something to do with Vietnam's revival, according to Wikipedia:

"Vietnam has been, for much of its history, a predominantly agricultural civilization based on wet rice cultivation. However, the Vietnam War destroyed much of the country's agrarian economy, leading the post-war government to implement a planned economy to revitalize agriculture and industrialize the nation.

"Vietnam's chief trading partners include China, Japan, Australia, other Asian countries, the United States and Western Europe. In 2011, Vietnam's total international trade, including both exports and imports, was valued at approximately $200 billion."

It's a weird feeling for a Vietnam veteran to walk into a shoe store and see the words "Made in Vietnam" etched into the heel of a sneaker. Weird in a good way. It is nice to know we didn't ruin Vietnam. Nice to know it is surviving on its own, just the way Ho Chi Minh would have liked, except for the free-market thing.

My group of Army veterans held reunions in Las Vegas in 2007 and again in 2009. We met at Bill Kimball's retirement home in Galena, Illinois during the summer of 2010. We were becoming friends in a modern sense of the word, communicating by phone and email from time to time. Jon Ringer and I conversed often, sharing our common interest in college sports while exchanging thoughts on these "new friends" we had caught up to in recent years.

"Seeing you guys at the reunion in 2007 was one of the greatest things ever in my life," Ringer said in an email one day. We were all glad to see Jon, too. While rounding up participants for the 2003 reunion, I had searched for a "Jon Ringer" on-line, found one in Iowa, where Jon had grown up, and made the phone call.

"Is Jon Ringer there?" I asked the voice that came on the phone.

"You mean my dad," the voice said.

"Yes."

"He died 10 years ago."

Oops. I didn't stay on the phone long to prolong the agony. We went on with our first reunion, thinking Ringer had passed to the Great Beyond.

Three years later, the real Jon Ringer found us on the Internet through the 2/32 website, and sent me an email. I had to tell him we thought he was dead and that's why we didn't invite him to the first reunion.

"Well, I'm not dead," he said, showing the same ironic sense of humor we knew from our days in Vietnam. "When's the next reunion?"

And that's how we came to hold our 2007 reunion, featuring the same group of guys along with a couple of wives.

In 2010, Kimball located Dean Vincent, one of the legendary people from Bill's tour, and we decided to meet again. Another reunion came together in Las Vegas during April of 2013. Kimball kept us laughing with his smooth joke-telling skills. Mike Niesius, fully recovered from a stroke he suffered in 2002, smiled as he talked about his role as the "fixer" of any mechanical issues that arose. Jon Ringer touched us all with an emotional speech to his war-time brothers as we ate dinner in a Vietnamese restaurant located in the lobby of the Treasure Island hotel.

My newspaper instincts had finally led me to the Military Page in January of 2011. We published those pages every Monday through Veterans Day in early November before dwindling responses led me to end the experiment. We ran over 1,000 photos of local veterans and featured at least 20 with personal stories told in their own words. Reporting those stories, and seeing so many photos of young soldiers who headed off to war, my pride in being a veteran came into the forefront of my life, cut loose from the shadows where it had lingered for nearly five decades.

My newspaper career came to a sudden halt in February of 2012 when I was "downsized" out of my job. I was nearly 65 years old and ready to retire. With too much time on my hands, I began to go back and read some of the Military Page stories. The next chapter tells the best of those stories. Hearing these veterans reflect on their years in the military had struck a chord with me. These veterans of past wars taught me the true meaning of taking pride in service to our country.

CHAPTER THIRTEEN: VETERANS' STORIES

ANTHONY STANIS

(Anthony Stanis fought in the Pacific Theater during World War II and has a clear memory of everything. One of his nephews urged me to call Anthony on the phone in 2011 and I got more than I could handle from an old soldier with total recall of his time in the Army nearly 70 years ago.)

Anthony Stanis can still look back clearly over the years, back to when he was young and a soldier in World War II.

"I ended up working in intelligence and reconnaissance," Stanis, 91 years old, said in the winter of 2011. "I got drafted into the Army on April Fool's Day, 1942. We did a lot of training all over the states. We were learning how to fight in the desert because that's where the fighting was over in North Africa. But then the Germans sank a couple of troop ships and we got delayed. In the meantime, we knocked the Germans out of North Africa. The Army sent us to West Virginia, into the mountains, so that we could train to fight in Italy.

"We learned how to rappel up the hillsides. We slept on the ground, did all the training every day, and then in around December of 1943 we got word to forget all this training. We were in the Navy now. They took us over to Norfolk, Va. We learned how to get up on a ship using the ropes. No more mountain training for us. Now we were being trained for amphibious landings. We were being prepared to go fight in the Pacific.

"After about a month's training in the Chesapeake Bay, we made a practice landing or two, and then they put my unit on trains to California. We took a ship to Hawaii and did more training there. We got to Guam in July of 1944. There were no planes on Guam. The Japs didn't have air cover either. We just fought each other like cowboys and Indians on Guam.

"I was with the 77th Intelligence Division, attached to the 305th Marines. We were a special platoon of around 22 soldiers who did scouting work, intelligence and reconnaissance. We would go out and scout one area or another on the island, making sure there were no surprises for our guys. I became a Platoon Sergeant. We had an officer to lead us, but they never lasted long. The first one only lasted one day and then took a medical leave. We never saw him again.

"As soon as we secured Guam, we were supposed to go to New Zealand for some R&R (rest and relaxation). But (General) MacArthur was heading back to the Philippines and he put in a bid for more troops. He was sort of in charge of both the Navy and the Army when it came to big decisions in the Pacific. So they turned our ship around. We said to hell with New Zealand and off we went to the Philippines.

"MacArthur used us to hit the beach on the southern part of Leyte Island. We landed just ahead of a Jap convoy that was bringing in more troops. As soon as we landed, there was a lot of fighting. I never got wounded, but I was close a lot of the time to getting hit. I was pretty lucky, I guess. Every night you were alone in a foxhole. There were soldiers in foxholes all around you, but you were still alone in the dark with your knife and your carbine, waiting for any Japs who infiltrated our lines. You always had a couple of hand grenades ready. I did a lot of praying. You stayed alert all night.

"We had the Japs bottled up in the mountains when word came that the Navy was going to Okinawa to fight that battle. They sent some LCTs in to pick us up and by March 26, 1945, we were landing in Okinawa, five days ahead of the invasion."

(We should interrupt Anthony's story here to mention the scale of this invasion. The battle for Okinawa was actually bigger, in some respects, than the Normandy Invasion in June of 1944 that kicked the Germans out of France. More than twice as many troops landed on the first day at Okinawa than were put ashore at the various landing beaches in France. The Navy suffered 5,000 men killed on Okinawa. Over 10,000 were knocked out of action. The Americans absorbed nearly 62,000 casualties in all. Approximately 12,000 were dead or missing in action. There were 120,000 Japanese soldiers on the island. By the end of the battle, 100,000 Japanese were dead, counting civilian casualties, many of them suicides. Okinawa was the last major battle of the Pacific Theater.)

"We finished fighting on Okinawa in June," Stanis continued. "Shortly before the fighting stopped, we started getting replacements. Prior to that, all replacements went to Europe.

"From Okinawa, we went to Cebu in the Philippines to train for the invasion of Japan, which was scheduled for November 5. We trained until August, when the Atom Bomb was dropped. When that happened, we had a big party. We drank 'Philippine Tuba,' which came from the juice located in the top of coconut trees. Most of the guys celebrated. Dropping the bomb probably saved one million lives. That's how many soldiers it was estimated we would have lost in an invasion of Japan. Unfortunately, the Japanese had to pay for it.

"From Cebu, we shipped to Otaru, Japan as occupation forces in October. We were greeted by a Japanese party in morning coats and top hats. It was decided we would not have to scout adjacent to the roads through Sapporo to a huge Army Base at Asahikawa. The Captain, who was the Occupation Officer, left me with two men and proceeded to go talk to the civilian authorities. Before he left, he handed me an American flag and ordered me to raise it, replacing the Japanese flag. We had to march out in front of all of these Japanese citizens and raise our flag. That was a real Flag Day, perhaps my proudest moment of the war.

"I got home in December of 1945, just before Christmas. My family still lived in the Bishop's Bend section of Pawtucket, down by the river. The cemetery came right up to our backyard. I had three sisters and a brother and we were all home for Christmas. I think that was the happiest Christmas of my life."

(*EPILOGUE: Anthony Stanis married Dorothy Harper after the war ended and raised four children – Mike, Christine, Dottie and Steve. He worked for over 30 years before retiring from the U.S. Army Map Service. His goal is to live until he turns 105.*)

BILL DONNELLY

(Infantryman Bill Donnelly used Vietnam as a measuring stick, saying "No matter how bad things got in my life ... it can't be as bad as Vietnam.")

PAWTUCKET – Bill Donnelly has done a pretty good job of putting Vietnam in his rear-view mirror.

"I came home from the war and went right back to where I was before," said Donnelly, a former rifleman with the 196th Light Infantry Brigade. "I was a kid from Pawtucket Vocational who played a lot of sports and was having a good time when I got drafted. I returned home two years later, resumed playing basketball and softball, and began my own printing business."

Donnelly had a lot of difficult Vietnam memories to suppress. He threw himself into his work and his sports outlets.

"What I had seen in Vietnam, there was no use trying to explain to people when I came home," he said. "If they can't hear and feel and smell Vietnam the way we did, they would never understand what I was talking about. You had to be there."

Along with more than two million other Americans of his generation, Donnelly got a letter in the mail, requesting his presence in the military machine that the government was expanding for a major war in Vietnam.

"I got drafted in September of 1965," Donnelly recalled. "I had been working for the Paramount Card company in the printing department before I got drafted. I was inducted on Oct. 19 and reported to Fort Dix. Then I was sent to Fort Devens, Mass., for basic training. That's where they were forming the 196th, a special unit of light infantry. By light infantry, I mean we would have no tanks with us.

"Very few of us knew much about Vietnam," Donnelly added. "Remember, this was 1965. The United States was dealing with a flare-up in the Dominican Republic and everyone thought we might go there. I went home on leave in the summer of 1966 and when I got back, we had our orders for Vietnam. Some of us had to look on a map to see exactly where Vietnam was located.

"We boarded a troop transport ship in Boston and sailed through the Panama Canal. Then we sailed up to Long Beach, California, where they reloaded the ship. We stayed there two nights and then we sailed across the Pacific. It took us 30 days to reach Vietnam."

Donnelly smiled at the memory of that ocean voyage.

"I always said I spent more time on the ocean than some of the guys who were in the Navy."

Donnelly's 196th LIB set up camp in Tay Ninh, a province capital about 50 miles northwest of Saigon and no more than eight miles east of the Cambodian border and the famed Ho Chi Minh Trail, a supply line for soldiers and supplies used by the North Vietnamese army.

"The camp wasn't even ready yet," Donnelly said. "We all went on sand bag details. Later, we started going out on operations. The 196th participated in operations called Attleboro, Gadsen, Cedar Falls and Junction City One and Two. We went all through the Hobo Woods and the Iron Triangle. My unit lost 50 percent of the guys I started out with over there.

"The first time we got pinned down, you wonder how you're going to get out of there. It's nothing like the war movies we used to watch back home. I talked to an officer one day and 30 minutes later he was dead. It just didn't seem real. As a soldier, you really started to appreciate everything about life back home."

Donnelly doesn't speak to any specific details about Vietnam. Guys who have seen a lot of combat tend to block it out rather than sit around telling stories to their buddies back home about what they had seen in the war. He speaks in general terms, in a quiet voice, when asked direct questions about Vietnam, but there are things he's just not going to talk about.

"I suppressed my memories about Vietnam," he said. "I felt so glad and lucky to get out of there alive. I saw so many people who were unlucky and did not come home. They were the heroes. When I got home (in 1967), I felt sorry for the kids I knew who had to go over there."

The war would last until 1975. All the while, Donnelly played softball and ran his printing business shop on Central Avenue.

"I used Vietnam as a crutch," he said. "No matter how bad things got in my life, I said it can't be as bad as Vietnam. Going to war makes a man out of you, that's for sure.

"I didn't get involved with any veterans' organizations until I was around 45 years old," he said. "I'm a member of the Vietnam Vets Chapter 818 in Cumberland. I am a past commander of the Eugene T. Lefebvre Post 1271. I've been a District 5 commander of the VFW and a past state commander of the VFW. I'm also a member of Disabled American Veterans."

Donnelly lists his involvement with veterans' organizations for a very definite reason.

"I think every veteran should register with the VA," he said. "Just go down to the VA Hospital in Providence and sign up. A lot of veterans don't even know what benefits they can receive by joining the VA.

"The VA will put you in a priority category. Every veterans' organization has a service officer who will interview you and find out what benefits you qualify for. They can help out vets who are out of work or are ill.

"My advice to any vets not in the system is to visit the local VFW, DAV, Purple Heart, American Legion or Vietnam Veterans organization and talk to their service officer," Donnelly added. "If you have a problem, they will help you out. For free. Go down to the VA office on Westminster Street in Providence. The DAV is located there, too. They have great service officers who help out veterans all the time."

Donnelly's serious demeanor lightens when he speaks about veterans helping veterans. Vietnam is just a distant memory for him now. Helping fellow veterans is something that drives him 45 years later.

"If I can lead veterans to people who can help them out, then I feel pretty good about myself," he said.

GEORGE PATRICK DUFFY

(George Patrick Duffy's story sheds light on destroyer escort duty served by seafaring sailors like himself during World War II off the coast of North Africa.)

PAWTUCKET – George Patrick Duffy's name is well-known around this city, most commonly associated with the 70 years he has spent coaching youth sports. What many people don't know is that Duffy endured a frightening experience while serving in the Coast Guard during World War II.

The white-haired gentleman sat in his living room back in 2011 and answered questions about his military career, speaking in the measured tones he developed while serving as publicity director for the old Providence Steamrollers and radio announcer for the Rhode Island Reds.

"I got out of high school in 1940," he began. "Went to work at the old H&B machine company in South Attleboro, packaging 75 millimeter shells for the British government. In April of 1942, I was walking around in downtown Providence and heard somebody call my name. It was Ray Coulombe, who had played ball against me in high school. He was now a recruiter for the Coast Guard. On April 20, 1942, I joined the Coast Guard."

Duffy was stationed in New England for a year.

"I ended up in a lighthouse in Chatham," he said. "There were security concerns with our coastline. We had Coast Guard personnel in Boston, Provincetown, Chatham, looking for any activity. I came home one day and said, 'I can't do this anymore. I have to volunteer for sea duty.'"

Duffy ended up in Texas on the crew of the newly commissioned USS Menges, a destroyer escort ship bound for duty in the European Theatre of war.

"My job was to man a 20-millimeter anti-aircraft gun on the starboard side of the ship," Duffy recalled. "I also worked the depth charge rack. Our mission was to escort cargo and troop ships to North Africa. The ocean was filled with ships as the buildup for the invasion of Europe began."

In April of 1944, the Menges and its crew rescued 128 sailors from the USS Lansdale, which came under attack from German airplanes and submarines in the water off North Africa. On May 3, the Menges was 15½ miles astern of its convoy, chasing down a radar contact when it was hit at 1:18 in the morning by a torpedo explosion so violent that the back third of the ship was destroyed, killing 31 and wounding 75.

"People were crying and yelling," Duffy recalled. "A friend of mine was cut in two when hit by a washing machine that was knocked free of its mooring and slid down the deck like a human knife. The ship tilted and began taking on water. We were preparing to abandon ship but Commander McCabe waited and the ship hung on. The steel that got twisted from the explosion swept upwards and prevented water from coming in.

"We got an SOS out and then just floated in the water like a cork," Duffy continued. "The big fear was that a German sub would surface and blow us away with its deck guns. But fortunately that never happened."

The Menges was taken in tow the next day and went back for repairs. Its front two-thirds that survived the torpedo were welded together with the back third of another ship that had been torpedoed in its front end, with a new ship emerging from the process.

Duffy and some of his crew mates landed in a hospital in Long Island where they stayed for two or three months, he recalled. The war was over for them.

"The scene the night we were torpedoed stayed in my mind for a long time," Duffy said. "I came home and began to put my life back together. I got a job doing publicity for the Providence Steamrollers and sat in on the second meeting held when the NBA was forming. I later became play-by-play announcer for the Rhode Island Reds hockey team. My life was back on track, but I don't think you ever really forget your war experience. It comes back to me sometimes. I was fortunate to come home."

Helen Duffy, who married George back in 1944, had been sitting quietly until now.

"Remember that fellow who worked for the restaurant on Federal Hill?" she asked. "What was his name? He was one of the 128 sailors you rescued and he was so grateful. We had dinner with him at his restaurant."

George Patrick Duffy nodded.

"He ended up as part-owner of the restaurant," Duffy commented.

"Did he pay for your dinner?" someone asked.

"No, I don't think so," Duffy recalled with a laugh.

GLORIA VIGNONE

(Gloria Vignone, an Army nurse in Iraq for two years, compares her war-time work to an emergency room at a city hospital.)

Gloria Vignone admits to feeling "bittersweet" about her tour as a nurse in Iraq back in 2006-07.

"Sometimes when you are here, you want to be there, and vice versa," the Franklin, Mass., native was saying back in the spring of 2011. "The camaraderie with your fellow soldiers is unbelievable. All we saw were trauma cases over there, a lot of blood and amputated limbs. We had one soldier who lost 60 units of blood and he lived. His buddies came in and donated blood to save his life. To know that you helped save a soldier's life is a feeling you never forget."

Now a full Colonel in the Army Reserves, Vignone is employed in civilian life as a nurse who works as a quality improvement educator at Sturdy Memorial Hospital in Attleboro, Mass. She spends one weekend per month with her reserve unit and 14-29 days on active duty each year. Her military assignment currently is at Fort Devens, Mass., where she serves as interim commander of the 399th Combat Support Hospital.

DUAL CAREER – Gloria Vignone joined the Army Reserve in 1988 and eventually served in Somalia and Iraq. She holds a Master's Degree in Nursing and balanced her private career with life in the Reserves.

Vignone was living in Johnston, R.I., back in 1988, possessor of a Master's Degree in Nursing, when she made a crucial life decision.

"I joined the Army Reserve in November of 1988," she recalled. "The reason I joined? I was thinking about another income and didn't know if Social Security was going to be around. I didn't discuss my decision with anyone. My mother was upset when I told her. My father thought it was great. He is a retired World War II veteran.

"Nothing was going on in the world when I joined the Army," Vignone said. "We were in between wars. My recruiter said, 'Don't worry. You will not have to go to war.'"

Vignone went into the Army with the rank of First Lieutenant, based on her Master's Degree. She volunteered for a peacekeeping mission in Kosovo in 2001, during the conflict between neighboring countries Serbia, Albania and Yugoslovia.

"I had never seen injuries like the ones we saw in Kosovo," said Vignone, who worked as head nurse of an intermediate care ward. "We saw heads bashed in, people all disfigured. It was a war zone and there was brutal fighting going on. Sometimes, we got caught in the middle. We always went places under armed guard.

"We were in Kosovo when 9/11 happened," Vignone added. "We had two weeks left in our mission before going home. My brother Tony lived in New York City and it took some time before I learned he was okay."

The innocent world of 1988 had changed drastically over the 13 years since Vignone joined the Army Reserves. The tragedy of 9/11 signaled the beginning of an ongoing war against terrorism launched by the Bush Administration.

Vignone was activated for Iraq in 2006.

"I was originally stationed in Mosul," she said. "When we got off the plane, the place was under mortar attack. That was our wake-up call. I knew we weren't in Kansas anymore! We would get mortared three or four times a week, usually around 3 in the morning. We had several mass casualty situations. At times, we were doing surgery in the Intensive Care

Unit. We couldn't keep up with the demand of wounded patients that needed the OR. These were all types of patients including U.S. soldiers, POWs and civilians.

"The wounded came in by ambulance," Vignone continued. "After an improvised explosive device went off, we had a civilian come in and complained of pain in his groin. He had a rib lodged there and the X-ray showed it was not his rib so it had to come from someone else.

"When we were stationed in Al Asad, the wounded could only come in by helicopter. The weather dictated when the wounded could be shipped to Germany or back home. The sandstorms were just impossible to deal with. Everything turns orange in a sandstorm and a hot wind is constantly blowing. It feels like a hairdryer blowing in your face. Somebody measured the temperature of the tarmac and it was 149.5 degrees.

"We treated mostly Iraqi army, civilians, POWs and U.S. soldiers," she said. "We had eight mass casualty situations and did a lot of surgeries. The doctors and nurses worked as a team and saved so many lives. Soldiers are better equipped today to stop bleeding or hemorrhaging by carrying tourniquets in their packs and placing them on the affected limb.

"Iraq was the dustiest and dirtiest place I had ever seen. The temperature would be 120 degrees by 1 in the afternoon. I found myself missing my family, my friends back home, and all the simple things of life. People would send us food by mail and we would make a pizza out of it. Sometimes my buddy, Colonel Luz, would barter for steaks, hamburgers and chicken and we would invite everyone for a cookout. At times we would have to put 30 steaks and hamburgers in our little dorm size refrigerator so we spread the "wealth" around a lot because having a steak, hamburger or pizza on the grill with your buddies was just awesome, even though it was with a non-alcoholic beer. Your boots are always muddy so I had a friend send me a brush. We had eight latrines and they would overflow often."

Vignone came home in 2007 and tried to transition back to civilian life, in between her stints with the Reserve unit.

"I absolutely see life with a different perspective now," she admitted. "It is all very sobering, to realize what our soldiers are going through. My own personal feeling is I think everyone in our country should do some sort of community service, to give back the way our soldiers do."

Working at Sturdy Hospital, Vignone occasionally sees traffic in the Emergency Room that reminds her of a war zone. "You never erase those memories of the ones you helped save and the looks on those faces that you couldn't save."

"Emergency rooms at hospitals in big cities probably are a better comparison," Vignone said. "In Iraq, you suddenly had casualties coming in and everyone was flying around, trying to do their jobs. I find myself thinking of my time in Iraq when I am home. You never really forget it, but you are proud you did it."

JIMMY BRENNAN

(Just a few months before he died in 2011, Jimmy Brennan looked back on the path of his youth that led him to the Philippine Islands just in time for World War II.)

PAWTUCKET – Jimmy Brennan graduated from St. Raphael Academy in 1936 at the height of the Depression. Four years later, as Hitler's army overran much of Europe, the United States revived its military draft.

"I was going to beat the draft," Brennan, 91, said. "I enlisted in December of 1940. The way the draft worked in those days, if they drafted you, you could end up in the Army for 10 years, either active or in the reserves. So I enlisted in the Army for three years.

"It was kind of comical, really, how it turned out. I originally enlisted so that I could join the cavalry outfit in Panama. If I had been accepted for the cavalry, I would have rode the war out in Panama. But when you signed up in those days, they gave you a 10-day leave, and before my 10 days were up, the enlistment sergeant came back to me and said they were looking for guys to join the Army Air Corps.

"That's how I ended up in the Philippines," Brennan added. "I went there in 1941. The Japanese knocked out the Air Corps before the year was out. General (Douglas) MacArthur put some of us Air Corps personnel in the provisional infantry. When the Japs put the pressure on, the government evacuated MacArthur and a lot of other key personnel. They took out the pilots, the navigators, the bombardiers. Me, I was just a clerk typist and a private. I stayed in the infantry.

"We were forced to exist on half-rations for three months before MacArthur was evacuated," Brennan recalled. "We were low on rations because when Manila was declared an open city, we didn't protect our store of rations. We were half-dead from starvation after three months on short rations. We had no medicine. We learned how to scavenge for whatever we needed.

"When the Japanese took control of the island, I didn't make the Bataan Death March. I was put in the hospital because I was so sick. I had lost 60 pounds. I was six feet tall and weighed 130 pounds. I was incarcerated in a hospital. The Japs put all their big guns around the hospitals and then used them to fire on Corregidor (where the last remnants of the American forces under General Wainwright were still holding out). The Americans and Filipinos wouldn't fire back because they didn't want to hit the hospital where so many prisoners were locked up.

"The Japs were smart. They were good strategists and great soldiers. The greatest glory in the world to them was dying for their Emperor (Hirohito). American soldiers just wanted to get the job done and go home. We didn't want to die for anyone. We wanted to live.

"I was a POW for 3½ years," Brennan added. "I spent 1½ years in the Philippines. Then I went on a 'Hell' ship to Japan. 'Hell' ships were unmarked freighters that often were sunk by American planes or ships because they appeared to be Japanese freighters. I was fortunate enough to survive the journey to Japan. I worked in a steel mill for two years. They kept us in a big room in a warehouse with just one Army blanket to share. It was cold in the winter and we had to huddle together to share our body heat.

"When the Armistice was signed in August of 1945, we were still working in the steel mill. We didn't get out of there until October. I spent a year in the hospital before I was able to get out of the Army and come home.

"It took me some time to get adjusted after I got home," Brennan said. "I worked for 33 years on the Pawtucket police force, ending up as a lieutenant. I retired 29 years ago, when I was 62 years old."

Brennan still lives in his own home, and his mind is sharp as ever.

"I forgave the Japanese a long time ago," he said. "It wasn't in me to hold a grudge. I've gone on with my life. Nowadays, I don't get out much, but I do attend a dinner with other veterans at the Gatchell Post on the last Thursday of each month. I would do anything for veterans of this country. We can't do enough for our veterans, if you ask me. America is No. 1 because of its veterans."

JOE DOMINGOS

(Joe Domingos found the grave of his brother Augustine on the island of Okinawa back in 1945).

PAWTUCKET – It seems like every person who lived through World War II has a story to tell. The war impacted everyone in the country back in the 1940s. Young men were drafted or enlisted in the military. Some able-bodied men worked in essential jobs and were required to continue in those jobs to help produce war materials for use by our Armed Services.

Women moved into the work force, too, gaining a foothold in the working world that they would never lose.

Parents and other family members went on with their lives, checking the newspaper each day for news from the European and Pacific Theaters.

They were on a vigil, waiting for the mailman to deliver letters from their soldiers, pinning stars to the front doors of their home to signify how many soldiers came from this household.

The Domingos family on Pleasant Street in Pawtucket sent three boys into the military. The oldest, Augustine, joined the Army in 1941. "Auggie" was 22 years old at the time. Brother Norbert joined the same year at the age of 17. Younger brother Joe was just 14 when the Japanese bombed Pearl Harbor and the U.S. entered the war. He would enlist in the Navy when he turned 17 in 1944.

"My brother Auggie had a friend who grew up on Pleasant Street, a guy by the name of Joseph Fernandes," Joe Domingos recalled. "He saw action with my brother. Both were in the 77th Infantry Division and they ended up fighting during the invasion of Okinawa. This was in 1945. I was in the Navy by then.

"Both Auggie and Joe (Fernandes) were badly wounded in action on Okinawa," Joe Domingos recalled. "Auggie died from his wounds. Joseph was shipped home. He went to our house and explained to my mother what happened to Auggie.

"I was on the USS Lejeune and we were anchored off of Okinawa. I was able to go ashore and look for my brother's grave. I came to a cemetery that had what seemed like thousands of little white flags on the graves. It took me a couple of hours to find Auggie's grave. But I found it. Seeing Auggie's grave made me very sad."

Auggie Domingos and many other American soldiers killed on Okinawa remain in the U.S. cemetery on that tiny island in the Pacific, one not far from Japan that served as a crucial victory for the Allies.

"My mother wanted Auggie to stay there," Joe Domingos said. "It was just all too painful for her."

Norbert Domingos returned home from the war in 1945 and died in 1998. Joseph Fernandes lived a long life, dying recently at the age of 95.

Joe Domingos worked for many years at the Newport Textile company. Now 83 years old, he is retired and living in Central Falls.

"I see your Military Page and it brings back many memories for me," he said. "You had a picture of George Patrick Duffy in the paper. He lived a couple houses away from us on Pleasant Street in Pawtucket before the war. The war really changed our lives.

"I still think of Auggie from time to time," Joe Domingos said. "He always took care of me and, being the oldest, he took care of our family too. Some nights I dream about Auggie. He was a real peach."

(Joe Domingos passed away late in 2012.)

JOHN COSTA

(John Costa and his two brothers, Joe and Francis, all served in World War II. Joe was killed by the Japanese in 1943 while carrying wounded American soldiers through the jungles of the Solomon Islands.)

PAWTUCKET – John Costa is 89 years old now and still lives in the house on Crane Street that he grew up in during the 1920s and 1930s.

"We had nine people in this house … my mother and father, five boys and two girls," the World War II veteran related back in 2011. "My twin sister Rose and I are the only ones still living. Rose lives out in Rehoboth."

Costa joined the National Guard in 1940, at the age of 18, admittedly "looking for a little excitement."

"I heard they had a year's worth of training scheduled in Florida," he said. "In those days, none of us could afford to drive to Florida. I joined the Guard and by 1941, I was in the full-time Army, working as a medic."

When the Japanese attacked Pearl Harbor, Costa's two brothers followed him into the service.

"Joseph was drafted in 1942 and ended up in the same unit as me – the 118th Medical Battalion," John Costa recalled. "He was in Company B and I was in Company C. Then our brother Francis joined up in 1943. He served with the 656th Field Artillery Battalion in Europe."

John Costa's unit was sent to the Solomon Islands in the Pacific in 1942. Joe ended up in the same region. He was killed by the Japanese in a horrible manner on July 18, 1943.

"During the Munda Campaign, Joe was with the group bringing our wounded, mostly litter cases, through the jungle. They were attacked by Japanese forces and they had no protection," John Costa said.

"The wounded, plus the medics, were massacred by the Japanese with bayonets, machetes and hand grenades. They all died a horrible death."

John Costa learned of his brother's death when a fellow soldier spotted Joe's name on a company bulletin board that listed recent Killed in Action reports.

"He showed me Joe's name and I said that must be him," John Costa recalled. "It was very sad for me. Joseph was always the favorite brother in our family. I could never forget Joe. I think about him all the time."

Brother Francis came home from Europe and lived a full life, passing away in 2008.

John Costa worked in electronics for many years.

"I was a radio engineer on the staff at WNRI in Woonsocket and also at WPAW in Pawtucket," he said. "There was no money in that. I ended up working for Raytheon in the Electronics Division."

Costa mailed in photos of his brothers and himself for use in the Military Page, proud to show the commitment his family made to the war effort.

"I sure did think of life a lot differently when I came home from the war," said the man who first joined the National Guard "looking for a little excitement."

ROLAND CARROLL

(U.S. Marine Roland Carroll met his future wife, Doris Smith, in downtown Pawtucket back in 1944, right before he got orders for the Pacific Theater.)

Roland Carroll never liked to talk about his World War II experience as a Marine who fought on Iwo Jima in the early months of 1945 while U.S. forces closed in on Japan.

"Who am I to talk?" the 88-year-old veteran admitted in 2011 when put on the spot. "I figured I wasn't the only guy who went in the service. We all had to go fight the war. I realize now how important it was. We had to win that war or Hitler and the Japanese were going to take over the world."

Carroll grew up in West Warwick, joined the Marines in 1942, came home and married Pawtucket native Doris Smith. They raised three daughters, and enjoyed a nice retirement in Florida until returning home a few years ago to be with their children and grandchildren.

"I didn't want to go in the Army," he recalled. "I preferred the Marines. They were in on all the action. I took basic training at Parris Island and then got assigned to Newport, R.I., where about seven of us provided security around the torpedo station. We used to take ferry-boat rides and one day we ended up in Pawtucket, walking around downtown."

WARTIME ROMANCE – Doris Smith met Army trainee Roland Carroll in Pawtucket midway through World War II and waited for him to come home from Iwo Jima before they got married.

Doris (Smith) Carroll picks up the story.

"I was mailing a letter with my sister Sally. We would go downtown to mail letters to servicemen. We came back from the Post Office and were standing outside Gibson's (a local restaurant). Roland was there with his buddies. They asked us if there was a place to dance nearby and we said there was, up the hill in Central Falls. We were going in that direction and showed them the way."

Roland follows the story intently and then proudly adds, "I was holding her hand by the time we got to the dance hall!"

Carroll would be transferred to the Pacific soon after, putting this budding relationship on hold for two years.

"In 1944, I went to Hawaii and then joined the Fourth Division," Roland said, resuming his story about life in the Marines. "I was in the infantry. They gave me an old O3 rifle and pretty soon I got an M1, which was the rifle everyone carried.

"My first real action came at Iwo Jima in April of 1945," Carroll added. "I was in a landing craft (when the invasion began). I was just a short guy and the landing door didn't go all the way down so one of the guys behind me just picked me up and threw me over the door, into the shallow water. I started going the wrong way at first. There was a lot of confusion and we were all carrying heavy equipment. A lot of guys drowned before they reached the beach.

"I ran up on the beach and got down between two soldiers. I give them the elbow to move and they were both dead. I high-tailed it out of there. Another time, I was in a foxhole with a little boy named Calvin. I told him not to leave the foxhole, but he got up and suddenly I had his blood all over me.

"The battle was very loud. The Japs had their artillery firing down on us from up on the hill. Iwo was only two miles wide and they were really dug in. Our ships were firing over our heads at the enemy. Some of the rounds fell short and hit our own troops. It was terrible.

"We were all very scared when we hit the beach, but you soon forget it. I was on Iwo for about three weeks. We saw the American flag raised on

Mount Suribachi. I caught a little bit of shrapnel in my leg from a shell that exploded near me.

"But what really hurt me was the blast concussion. What a strange feeling that was! The inside of my head went numb. I never remembered how they got me to the (field) hospital."

Carroll got out of the Marines later in 1945, cutting through all the red tape of the bureaucracy, passing up on military benefits due a Purple Heart campaigner so that he could get home and resume his civilian life.

"We got married in 1946," Doris Carroll said. "We settled down and raised our daughters, Sharlene, Donna and Debbie."

"Daddy got around $114 per month from the government for most of his life," daughter Deb Ruthowski pointed out. "We thought he deserved more, but we never really knew all that he went through because he never talked about his war experiences to us. We finally went to the VA and now he is getting more money for what he went through."

VA doctors have speculated that the concussive trauma of what Roland Carroll endured at Iwo Jima caused him to block out the memories for more than 50 years. Only after he suffered a minor stroke several years ago did Carroll start to speak more freely to his family about the war.

"We went to a funeral one time in Florida," Doris Carroll remembered. "The honor guard began playing Taps and I looked over at Roland and he was just bawling and hollering and crying all at the same time. We had to take him out of the funeral. We don't go to funerals any more. It's too difficult for him."

When Roland Carroll visits the VA these days, he wears his Iwo Jima hat that has the words "Uncommon Valor" emblazoned across its peak.

"The other veterans come up and salute Dad and shake his hand," Deb Ruthowski said. "They ask for his autograph sometimes. We have a picture of Dad that was taken with a Korean War vet and a Vietnam vet. They asked Dad to be in the photo."

Roland Carroll smiles gently as his daughter tells the story.

"There are not too many of us (WWII veterans) left," he said. "You wonder why you survived and some of your buddies didn't."

Deb's husband, Jim Ruthowski, lightens the mood with a final question.

"What was tougher: Going to war or raising three daughters?"

Roland Carroll smiles and thinks it over for a moment.

"That's debatable," he said, looking at his wife for support. "Raising three daughters wasn't easy!"

LEWIS SOARES SR.

(Lewis Soares Jr. describes his father's service to the United States during World War II.)

My father, Lewis Soares Sr., was born in Lisbon, Portugal and came to the United States when he was 3 years old. Because his father had died in Portugal, his mother remarried.

During his youth, he worked with his stepdad, who had a fruit and meat peddling business that was located in Pawtucket.

When he came of age in the late 1930s, my father made the decision to try and enlist in the Army when Europe was having its turmoil. He was denied enlistment because he was not a U.S. citizen. Shortly after that, he married in 1939 and went on to become assistant manager at the United Public Market of Pawtucket across from City Hall.

In 1943, his brother enlisted in the Army Air Corps, and in 1944 my father was drafted. At that time, my sister was 4 years, I was 2 years and my little sister was 3 months old.

My father at first was extremely upset. Being drafted with three small children was unfair, especially after he had tried to join when he was single. He also said at that time that if he had $500 cash, his name would have been placed on the bottom of the list of draftees. He felt that was unfair because only the extremely rich could afford the fee and he wasn't rich at all.

After being drafted and shipped overseas, one of the officers realized that my father was not an American citizen. That needed to be corrected before the ship landed. So while on board ship, my father became a citizen and his name was changed from Luis to Lewis Soares.

While serving in Naples, his brother, Frank Santos Sr., had already been in the Army Air Corps for about a year and did not know that his stepbrother, Lewis Soares, my Dad, had been drafted.

As my father's unit was preparing to leave Naples for another battle front, he met his brother Frank, who was with his battalion as refreshment troops. They did have an opportunity to talk about home and the horrors of war and at that time my father's picture was taken with him and two of his buddies, which was given to him after the war.

None of those in the picture survived except for my father. He always treasured that picture.

After coming home from the war, my father returned to United Public Market hoping to regain his old job as Assistant Manager. That was not to be. His job was reduced to nothing and the person he had trained became his boss (assistant manager).

Eventually, my father began his own successful grocery business. He was extremely proud to be an American Citizen and a Serviceman. He became a life member of the Amvets and VFW. When my father died, he was given full military honors and now rests in Swan Point Cemetery.

MIKE ROOSE

(Pawtucket Red Sox strength coach/trainer Mike Roose spoke in 2011 about how military service shaped his own life and dreams.)

PAWTUCKET – Mike Roose's active military career has been over for six years. He is 29 years old and an Air Force veteran who served in both Iraq and Afghanistan.

The Cumberland native is living a personal dream as strength coach for the Pawtucket Red Sox. But he can't quite put his military career behind him.

"I visited the VA (Veterans Administration) hospital in Providence during the off-season," Roose was saying before a PawSox game as players wandered in and out of the trainer's room. "I want to offer them my experience as a physical trainer. I want to work with veterans coming home from Iraq and Afghanistan, guys who may be battling PTSD or depression. The VA people told me that some medical studies have shown that exercise can help relieve depression. They are formulating a program that could offer exercise and other forms of therapy to veterans who need some help. I hope to be part of that program."

Roose appreciates how much four years in the Air Force shaped his life.

"I think my military service gave me the confidence and determination to chase my dreams," he said. "It was definitely helpful to me. When I went off to college, I really wasn't prepared for that challenge. After college, I joined the Air Force and when I came out four years later, I had a much better idea how to get things done. I would definitely recommend the military as an option for kids coming out of high school who aren't sure what they want to do with their next step."

Roose grew up in Cumberland and moved to Cape Coral, Florida when he was 16 years old. A solid baseball player, he ended up attending Mars Hill College in North Carolina, where he started at third base as a freshman before a broken foot sent him back to Rhode Island, where he attended classes at CCRI, still chasing his baseball dream.

And then 9/11 happened. Roose, not sure of his own future at this point, was so affected by the terrorist actions against this country that he joined the Air Force within two weeks of the national tragedy.

"I was moved, inspired," he recalled in an article written by *Pawtucket Times* sports writer Brendan McGair. "Everyone thought I was crazy."

Roose, 21 at the time, went through basic training in San Antonio, Texas before heading to an assignment in Georgia. He was sent to Iraq in 2003, just in time for the invasion that topped Saddam Hussein's government. Roose spent three months in Iraq and then six months in Afghanistan.

"I was trained to be an MP (Military Policeman)," Roose recalled last week. "But then I was selected for a counter-terrorism program. I went to Iraq with the 820th Special Forces group. Our duties included convoy security and protecting the air base from terrorists and rocket attacks. To do that, we had to gather intelligence from the area surrounding the base, which meant we had to go out into the neighborhoods, talking to people, trying to get to the terrorists who were making bombs or shooting rockets at our planes. We had to cut the head off the snake. We kicked down some doors when we were scooping guns off the street."

Roose seemed transported back in time as he talked about his year in the Middle East.

"I still miss the excitement of being in a war zone," he admitted. "I miss it a lot. You miss the friends you made, the teamwork that soldiers in combat develop. But I'm lucky because a baseball team is similar to the military. Soldiers and athletes both have similar goals. There are highs and lows during a baseball season, just as there are in a war zone. We travel together as a team, just like in the military. We build a bond as a team when we travel. Both soldiers and players keep things loose with a lot of humor. So there are similarities."

Roose understands that his military career, and his exposure to the adrenalin rush that exists within a war zone, have changed him as a person.

"I learned to appreciate everything about life a little bit more after serving overseas," he said. "My perspective on what is important has definitely changed. I came home and looked in the mirror and saw a stronger person than I had been before I went into the Air Force."

Roose left active duty with the Air Force in 2005, earned a degree in exercise physiology at Florida State in 2009, and landed back in Rhode Island with the PawSox just one year later. His military background proved to be a key factor in obtaining a job in Boston's minor league farm system. Pat Sandora, the minor league strength and conditioning coordinator for Boston, knew about Mike's Air Force career and where he had served. Three days after graduating from Florida State, Roose accepted a summer internship with the Red Sox that quickly turned into a job with Pawtucket.

After settling in with the PawSox, Roose is intent on helping veterans, many of them his age, who are having trouble making a transition back into civilian life.

"Giving back to veterans is something I want to do," he said. "I feel so helpless when I hear about veterans who can't deal with their problems when they come home. A couple buddies of mine went through that. Guys end up killing themselves because they are depressed and don't know the way out.

"If I can do anything to help veterans re-adjust, that would make me real happy," Roose said.

RONNIE BRISSETTE

(Woonsocket's Roger Brissette and his sister Vivian were kind enough to talk about their brother Ronnie, who was killed in Vietnam in 1966.)

Roger Brissette walked into the *Woonsocket Call* office in the spring of 2011 carrying details of his brother Ronnie's life. Roger's emotional words and gestures revealed how much a dead soldier from Vietnam would be missed, long after he had been put into the ground.

Roger and his sister Vivian never forgot their little brother Ronald, who got drafted in 1965, went to Vietnam a year later, and died during The Battle of Loc Ninh Plantation on June 11, 1966.

"I think about Ronnie every day," Roger, 72, admitted.

Vivian still battled bitter emotions over the loss of her brother, 45 years later.

"I guess that I would add only that the pain of the loss hasn't gone away," Vivian said. "Not one bit. ... I haven't really ever come to terms with it. I'm still angry on top of sad."

A combat friend of Ronnie got in touch with Roger in 1996, setting off a discovery process for the remaining Brissette family members.

According to the friend, Ronnie Brissette gave his life to save his buddies. An unauthorized report of the battle backs up this recollection:

"During the battle," the report began, "one grenade rolled next to PFC Ron Brissette, who although already wounded by the Viet Cong was still able to move and fire his rifle. He threw himself towards the man next to him, taking the blast from the grenade, thus saving the life of one of his friends. Seeing this, Spec. 4 Richard Mitchell stood up with his machine gun and started firing. The remaining members of the platoon began yelling at him to stay down. Mitchell didn't. Sgt. Hozy heard Mitchell say, 'It doesn't matter. We're all dead anyway.'"

Ronnie Brissette was one of 18 members of his company to die that day as the Viet Cong overran the Recon Platoon at Loc Ninh Plantation, which is more well-known for supplying the rubber that makes Michelin tires.

"I was at work the day we found out Ronnie had died," Roger Brissette recalled. "My dad and stepmom came to the company where I worked. I got a call to report to the personnel office. I remember my dad telling me Ronnie had died. I also remember having to walk back to my department, crying like a baby."

The Brissette family mourned their lost brother Ronnie. No family ever fills the hole left by the death of a young brother or sister. It was no different for the Brissettes. They eventually moved on with their lives, keeping Ronnie's memory close in their minds and their hearts.

Then the phone rang one day in 1996 at Roger Brissette's home.

"The guy on the other end asked if this was the family of Ronnie Brissette and I said, 'Yes, my son is Ronnie Brissette. He is named after his uncle who died in Vietnam.' This fellow said you're the guy I want to speak with. He told me we had a lot to discuss. Then he said he had been waiting to speak to Ronnie's family for 30 years. He said he was my brother's best buddy in their unit. I don't want to use his name in your story because I haven't been able to get him on the phone to get his permission. So let's just say he was Ronnie's best buddy."

The best buddy spoke to Roger of a religious medal Ronnie had given him back in Vietnam.

"He said one of the things that had been bothering him over the years was that Ronnie gave him a St. Christopher's medal to keep him safe. He said he had been carrying it for 30 years and felt guilty. He thought it should be returned to Ronnie's family. But I said no, Ronnie gave it to you as a friend. You keep it. That's probably why you are still around."

Roger Brissette and Ronnie's best buddy have kept in touch over the past 15 years. The friend has provided a wealth of information and anecdotes about his time together with Ronnie.

Ronnie Brissette was awarded the Purple Heart, the Military Merit Medal and The Gallantry Cross with Palm awarded by the Government of the Republic of Vietnam with this meritorious citation:

"Courageous combatants, well known for their sacrifices, who have always exhibited a spirit of good will and cooperation. They assisted the Republic of Vietnam Armed Forces in blocking the Red Wave of aggression from engulfing South Vietnam and Southeast Asia ... Some died in the performance of their missions. Their losses have been greatly mourned by both Americans and Vietnam comrades-in-arms."

Roger Brissette now knows so much more about his brother's time in Vietnam then he did back in July of 1966.

"The captain who escorted Ronnie's body home told us Ronnie died from multiple fragmentation wounds caused by a mortar shell exploding nearby," Roger said. "Ronnie's friend said that might have been true, but that the battle was so crazy, he thought it was a combination of the grenade and maybe even rifle fire along with the mortar that killed Ronnie. He was right in the trench with Ronnie. He said the mortar hit nearby, most of it hit Ronnie, who was between the mortar and himself. Then Ronnie dove on the ground when a grenade landed and saved the life of a sergeant.

"Ronnie's friend said the sergeant whose life Ronnie saved has completely buried the memory of that day and never talks about it," Roger Brissette said.

One thing we know for sure: Ronnie Brissette died while saving the lives of at least two of his fellow soldiers.

"Ronnie would be 67 years old now if he had survived the war," Roger Brissette said, wistfully.

THE PEOPLE LEFT BEHIND

A poignant moment in my newspaper career occurred in 2011 when a frail old woman walked into the *Woonsocket Call* newspaper office carrying a picture of her fiancé, who had been killed in World War II, nearly 70 years before.

"Please do not lose this photo," she said. "It is the only one I have of my dear Francis." We talked for a few minutes. She never married. "I could never forget Francis. He was the love of my life."

And then there was the woman who sent me an email telling a story about her father, a World War II veteran who had died in 1985.

"Dad passed away a month after returning from the 40th reunion they had with both the Japanese and U.S. soldiers on the island of Iwo Jima. It was the first time they did it, and there have been a few since. Anyway, one day many years later I googled my father's name to see what came up, and I found his name listed in a book of letters from guys in WWII.

"He was a student at Penn at that time and he, along with many of his fraternity brothers, enlisted in the service. They wrote letters back to a buddy who did the school paper. He, in turn, assembled all his buddies' letters and published a newsletter to all the guys so they knew what everyone else was up to. In 2001, a book with all the letters was published.

"I never knew my dad did this. If my mom knew, she never mentioned it. So there I sat, reading letters my father had written when he was 23 years old. His thoughts on the war, life, girls, along with lots of funny stories. What a wonderful gift!"

CHAPTER FOURTEEN: ORAL HISTORIES

(An oral history collected from soldiers who served in A Battery, 2nd Battalion, 32nd Artillery, in Vietnam between 1967 and 1969.)

TONY HOEHNER:

My thought about our time in Vietnam is always evolving because my study of Vietnam is always adding information that changes my perceptions. We were a damn good unit that took our jobs seriously. The memories of teamwork and camaraderie still echo in my consciousness. I would add that human males have a deep need to participate in some social strata. We approach that need in sports and fraternal organizations. But we evolved and came pre-wired to participate as warriors defending our tribe. That need is in our marrow. What separates us from the other social groups is the element of death and the danger that we faced. Even though we never had a ground attack at St. Barbara, any day there, or in convoy, could be our last. We faced mortars and mines. That element of danger supercharged our bonding. Add to that many hours of working together, we grew to know each other in a unique way. We never got to do that again, but remember when we did.

Years ago I read a statement by a British Naval officer who had served on a ship in the Atlantic where danger was omnipresent. He said when he first heard of the German surrender, he grew sad because he knew that he would never experience the closeness of the crew again. So it is with us. That is why we travel and long to be with one another once more at reunions.

JON RINGER

Most of us were draftees. We didn't ask to go. We were sent. Given a choice of avoiding the Army and later avoiding Vietnam, we probably would have chosen the easy way. And now ... as more and more time passes ... we often give the impression that it was our idea to go to war, live in a dirt hole with rats and dodge mortar attacks. Our idea to have spent a year in a country where at least 2 million people were trying to kill us.

While we were there, we tried to convince ourselves that "this isn't me." Back home, I don't wear a green suit, take orders from 20-year-old kids, or stay on the job 168 hours per week. Back home, I don't work for nine bucks a day, fill sandbags or stand in line for Spam and Kool Aid. Back home, I don't think a warm beer is a treat, an hour of silence is a bonus, or a hot shower is a dream. No, back home, I'm a big shot.

I don't know when I realized that no one was picking on me. Everybody had a different profile back home. And the only thing anyone had that was the same in Vietnam as it was in Huck-a-Buck, U.S.A. was our character. Jungle boots and steel pots don't change that.

I put it away for 40 years. Then I stumbled into 10 old soldiers who reminded me that it really did happen. And the last few years have made me realize that the year I spent in Vietnam had more impact on me than any other 12 months of my life. At 18 to 23 years old, we controlled tons of ordinance everyday ... dropping it on targets 10 to 15 miles away. We trusted each other and we trusted ourselves. I feel we were good soldiers (a title not to be taken lightly). And I truly believe we would have died for each other.

If someone else wants to feel shame or remorse for that war, let it be. I am proud of my service and the men of high character with whom I served.

MEL MAJOR

I had only been married for three months when I was drafted. I think Vietnam was the biggest factor in the failure of our marriage. I didn't realize how much I had changed. It was very hard to try and find what I had lost with the important people in my life. Not to mention the fact that everybody was two years ahead of me with their life. It seemed that most of the things we had in common two years prior were gone. It was an awkward time for me and them. But I am proud of my service in a top-notch artillery unit. "Steel on Target!" The friendships we made way back then have grown closer by the reunions we have had. It's all good.

BILL KIMBALL

I was drafted into the Army in September 1966, one month after my nineteenth birthday. Five months later I was headed to Vietnam, a country I knew little about and had no idea what to expect when I arrived. Even though many citizens opposed our nation's involvement in Vietnam, I personally felt I was performing an important and necessary service to my country by serving in the military. I was proud to serve as a soldier in the United States Army, and remain proud of my service to this day.

WE MEET AGAIN – Carl Miller, Bill Kimball and Tom Barrett served together in Vietnam and then met again 35 years later at the first FDC Reunion in Las Vegas.

During my tour in Vietnam, I was assigned to the fire direction center of a combat field artillery unit. It was a small section within an artillery battery that plotted targets and computed firing data for the guns. Although back then we made manual calculations, computers make the job much easier today.

While assigned to the FDC, I had the pleasure to meet and serve with many wonderful people (and some real characters) who worked extremely well together to fulfill a mission. Although there were about 100 soldiers assigned to our four-gun unit, with few exceptions it seemed as though FDC personnel chose to associate mostly with FDC section members. I think FDC personnel developed special bonds with fellow unit personnel. I found this to be true later in life when I became a police officer. Most law enforcement agencies are para-military organization and, as such, once one becomes a police officer it seems as though they develop special bonds and friendships with their fellow officers and tend to associate mostly with them, on and off duty.

Although I hadn't been in contact or seen some of my fellow soldiers in 35 years, we did manage to get in touch via the Internet and later meet in Las Vegas for a reunion. I didn't really know what to expect since I thought life had probably taken us all on different paths and wasn't sure how we would react to or accept each other. But I can honestly say that although we hadn't seen or contacted each other in many years, after being together for just five minutes, I felt like it had only been about a week since I last saw and talked with them.

LARRY KLEINSCHMIDT

I am a Vietnam veteran. I find that to be a big part of my identity, and inseparable from my "self" in every way. During a psychiatric evaluation I was asked what life would have been without Nam; if I could envision myself without it. I had never considered that before, but my answer was clear and quick. "I don't know, it has always been part of me." I cannot remember a day without many, many thoughts of Nam.

I do remember a "boy" flying out of Pierre, S.D. in 1968. As we passed over the great Oahe Dam, I looked down as long as I could, thinking to myself this may well be the last time you see this homeland, this beautiful country in which you were raised. It was not to be the last time I would set eyes on S.D., but it was the last time that "boy" was to be there, or anywhere else in this world. All of life would change over the next 16 months.

I struggled when I returned from Nam, as did most Nam vets. I couldn't talk openly about it. I couldn't "get ahead" as all the better jobs were held by those who had stayed in college, avoided combat and gotten a big start on the rest of us. Life was a struggle, even with the aid reluctantly offered by the VA. I eventually did get through college after years of slow progress, taking one or two courses at a time; my concentration had been seriously affected by the war. The war was a key part of my divorce, and a big issue as I fought for custody of my children. Derogatory terms like "baby killer" were thrown around the courtroom by attorneys who had spent the war years hiding out on college campuses. Such were the times in which we lived.

In the early years, I banded together with a few other Nam vets to form a VVA chapter. We struggled with the local politicians to win the right to have a Vietnam Memorial. I enjoyed the companionship of the Nam vets I knew, and the "struggle" seemed to be appropriate in a country which almost hated us for returning home alive. We were openly shunned by veterans of earlier wars.

Now in my later years, I find the companionship of the Nam vets I know to be especially cherished. I find that I am among a group of men who are brothers in a way which is stronger than birthright. I have special pride in the Proud Americans of the 2/32 Artillery, my brothers in arms from the Vietnam War.

After 40 plus years, I have open pride in my service, and my country has accepted me and my service. All my Nam vet brothers acknowledge each other with the warm greeting which was withheld from us for so long – "Welcome Home." My wonderful home state of South Dakota even threw a "welcome home" party for us, only 36 years after I returned; but better late than never!

Every veteran bears the burden of combat in his/her own way. Life goes on, but the burden never gets any lighter, never fades; it will be with me until my final breath.

JON RINGER

My year in Vietnam was broken into many phases of personal evolution. Ignorant and fearful ... cautiously confident ... not afraid, but not believing I'd ever go home ... a pretty good soldier ... ignorant and fearful.

Winston Churchill once said, "There is no more exhilarating feeling than being shot at and missed." Such an incident changes soldiers in two ways: It gives you a false feeling of superiority and invincibility. And it immediately shrink-wraps a lifetime bond between you and everyone in your presence.

The bond feels like this: "We dodged a bullet and maybe cheated death together. I needed my buddies to make it. And, maybe I helped them, too."

We didn't know it at the time, but at that moment we became lifetime members of a club. Nobody will throw you out. Like a tattoo or a house in Peoria ... you will have it for life.

The Boy Scouts, the high school sports team, and the college fraternity. Friendships in those organizations will be cherished forever. But the bond of combat ... even in a mild form ... makes brothers out of everyone in that proximity.

You may have had little, very little in common with this diverse group of 18- to 23-year-olds prior to that moment. And later, you may spend the rest of your life traveling another path. It makes no difference. You will always be brothers.

Once the year had passed and the jungle was a memory, I tried to return to who I was. Since it wasn't popular to be a soldier in the 1960s, I felt it best to only talk about it when asked. I would suggest the year was an aberration rather than a definition of who I was. That was incredibly wrong. I had become Vietnam though I lived in denial.

Forty years flew by. A 35-year newspaper career. A small but beautiful family. Lots of golf and ball games. All of it mixed in with the challenges of life we all face. Then I found a book with a reference I recognized. And a website with Terry Nau's name. And more names. Carl Miller and I had lunch. What a day! I found out that 10 of us who had shared two cramped bunkers had moved on to populate and inhabit virtually every corner of the United States.

My first reunion was powerful. Standing by the baggage claim in Las Vegas and watching a "sixty-plus" year-old man walk up with a different body, gray hair, and yet the same eyes and smile ... was emotional.

Over the year in the jungle, I learned too many things to list. Things about myself and life in general. I didn't acknowledge them for many years. But these last few years, I've found it introspective to open the time capsule and read the book.

There was a time when Vietnam was just a part of my personal and professional resume. Later, it became acceptable to talk and write about. I once agreed with Robert McNamara that it may have been just a waste of time. It wasn't a waste of time. It was part of the Earth's chronicle with both dark moments and virtuous acts. It may have been a short chapter in the history of struggle and conflict, but it had incredible social significance.

Today, I'm comfortable with my own definition of the war and my involvement. The United States kept a promise to an ally. Conscription was the law of the land, and I obeyed the law. If anyone says I should have been courageous enough to defy that law, they may not fully understand courage.

Vietnam was not for the timid. Twelve months in a small country where two million people are trying to kill you can be as tough as it sounds. Wars are only won when one side gets tired of being killed. The American public tired, but the American soldier was superior.

As we were unjustly scorned as soldiers in the 1960s, we are now a bit overly praised as old vets. Many of us went to war reluctantly and shouldn't pretend that it was our idea to go. Others did volunteer and were far braver than I could understand.

Being a soldier is an honorable vocation ... even as a temporary job. But, being a reliable comrade is a very fine character trait.

Mike Neisius was a good soldier and a good guy. He could build or fix anything. And did. He had no agenda except to do his job and someday go home. One night, an intense mortar attack knocked down the radio antenna on the roof of the FDC bunker. We had no external communications without it.

Without hesitation, Mike put on a flak jacket and a steel pot to go outside and climb to the roof. After some thought, Chuck Rosenblum reluctantly decided to go out and help.

Reluctance doesn't begin to describe my attitude. I stuck my head out and said, "Hey, you guys don't need any help, do ya?"

Mike yelled down, "We could use somebody to climb on top of the XO bunker with the guide wire to the antenna. Wrap it around a sandbag and stack a couple more on it to anchor it down."

"Would that someone have a green suit on?" I asked.

Three guys. One brave, one a bit cautious, but courageous enough to climb to the roof without being asked. And one who just didn't want to shame himself in front of his colleagues and friends.

Mike and Chuck righted the antenna, and I climbed to the roof of the other bunker with the wire ... wrapped it around a loose sandbag and secured it. As I finished, more mortars came in. We leapt off the 10-foot-high bunkers and scrambled inside.

Would I have died for them that night? Glad I didn't.

No, seriously, would I have died for them? On that night, I believe we would have made mutual sacrifices. And now. Today. If I am in the presence of one of those 10 men ... or anyone else who was in that jungle retreat known as French Fort in 1968 ... I am humbled.

And, I'm proud that they accept me as one of their own.

CARL MILLER

In December of 1965, my wife (now of 43 years) and I were engaged and planning our wedding. But in June of 1967, I received my draft notice for the Army. Having already lost a few classmates in Vietnam, it was my decision to postpone our wedding date. I couldn't imagine the possibility of leaving my future wife a young widow.

Twenty years old, scared, and not knowing what to expect, I reported to serve my country. Now as I look back on my time in the service, even in time of war, I realize how it prepared me for life beyond the military. My stint in the Army taught me to respect other people and support/trust others as I also wanted to be treated.

Our rigorous schedule of duties gave me a work ethic that helped me succeed in business. Living how and where we did in a country that really did not appreciate us gave me an appreciation for what we had after returning to the States.

And little did I know what the "fraternity" that I was drafted into would still mean to me 40 years later. I never realized how the friendships that were created in 1968 would continue to influence my life.

After many years of "silence" regarding that unpopular war and our experiences, we began to reunite our "band of brothers" and now feel good about sharing those experiences, not only with each other, but with family and friends as well.

MEL MAJOR AND ANDY BAILEY

Mel Major arrived at Camp Saint Barbara (aka French Fort) in March of 1968, reporting for duty as a cannoneer in Section 4.

"That was Sergeant Bolden's gun," Major recalled in 2013. "One of the first people I met was Andy Bailey. When a new guy comes in, people always ask him where he lives back in the States. Turns out Andy lived only 20 miles away from me in Michigan. He was from Davison and I came from Lapeer. We had lots to talk about right away."

FINAL TRIBUTE – Mel Major stands over tombstone of fellow Proud American cannoneer and good friend, Andy Bailey, during 2012 memorial service in Michigan. (Photo by GARY GOULD)

Cannoneers didn't have much time to themselves, due to a heavy daily work schedule.

"We would get up in the morning, have breakfast, and then start filling sand bags," Major said. "We filled a lot of sand bags. Then you had to do PM (preventive maintenance) on your own weapon. The whole crew had to perform PM on our big gun, either the 8-inch or the 175 millimeter. That was an important part of our routine.

"If you weren't filling sand bags, sometimes we would get an hour to ourselves after lunch," Major added. "At night, we either had guard duty or were firing H&Is. I remember when I first got to camp, I couldn't believe how loud the guns were when they fired. I wondered how these guys were able to sleep through all the noise but within a few days, I was sleeping through it, too. You were so dog-ass tired, so worn out, you get acclimated to just about anything, I guess."

Mel and Andy found a way to break the monotony of daily life.

"We both had Kodak video cameras," Major said. "The little Super 8s that were popular back then. I purchased mine in the PX at Tay Ninh base camp. I was there about two weeks and thought this is pretty good duty, hanging around a base camp, but then they put us on a convoy out to French Fort and things changed in a hurry."

The two Michiganders possessed a joy for living that proved infectious with their gun crew. They would be seen taking videos of themselves and their friends during work breaks. In one photograph that is part of Major's scrapbook, Mel is seen hanging from the end of a 175-mm tube, his legs wrapped around the long barrel, a big grin on his face.

"We had a lot of fun for a while," Major remembered.

Things changed for the worse on Sept. 18, 1968.

"Andy and Sgt. Bolden were part of a team that went outside our gate to help a 105-millimeter battery set up its guns," Major said. "They came under mortar attack. We had been getting a lot of incoming mortars over the past month but this one was pretty bad. We got word there were wounded (soldiers) outside the perimeter. We could hear the incoming rounds. Everybody came out of their bunkers. Someone came running over and said a bunch of guys had been hurt. Andy had the most serious wounds. Sgt. Bolden was hurt, too."

A medevac helicopter soon arrived to take the wounded back to Tay Ninh base camp. And that was the last Mel Major would see of his friend Andy Bailey until the following year.

"After I got home, Andy was convalescing at his aunt and uncle's house in Flint, Michigan," Major said. "At that point, his aunt called me up and said you gotta come over and see what Andy can do. I went over and they showed me. Andy could sit on the floor without falling over. He wasn't paralyzed from his wounds, but the injury prevented him from standing or sitting without falling over. So this was a big point in his recovery, his aunt told me. It progressed from there. She rehabbed him to the point where he could get up and stand on his own. And then he could take a step. It was a very slow process that took place, year after year."

Meanwhile, the videos that Mel and Andy had taken were stored away, just a memory of their time in Vietnam.

"My dad was a big photography nut," Major admitted. "I must have got that from him. I never realized those pictures and videos we took would be so important to me after I got home. But they were. I wanted some record of what me and Andy had been through. I got a hold of our cameras and took them to some guy in a video store who strung the videos together into a long film that we called 'Mel and Andy's Nam.' We gave a bunch of those films to soldiers we had served with."

Andy Bailey, 100 percent disabled by his wounds, fell in love with one of his caregivers.

"They got married," Major recalled, "but within a couple of years, she was diagnosed with a rare disease and died. Andy was pretty shook up. He moved to Florida to be closer to his father. Because he was disabled with a head injury, people began to take advantage of him. They took his money whenever his checks came in from the VA. Andy just sort of bounced around. We kept in touch through letters and phone calls, but there wasn't much I could do with Andy so far away."

Bailey died in 2006 and was buried back in his hometown of Davison, Michigan. Nobody got in touch with Mel Major to let him know his old friend had died.

"I found out in 2007," Major said. "I went to the cemetery where he was buried and couldn't find his grave. A guy working at the cemetery told me where Andy had been buried and showed me the grave. There was no headstone, not even a marker. Andy served his country and had been totally disabled by his wounds. I said 'Come on, man, this guy deserves a headstone.' I worked with the family to get a death certificate so I could try to get Andy a headstone, but nobody was able to help me.

"Finally, I got in touch with Larry Kleinschmidt, who had worked in Section One of our battery in Vietnam. We had communicated a few times before. Larry told me he got an email from Chuck Healey, who runs the website for the 2nd Battalion, 32nd Artillery, which was our old unit. Chuck knew of a marble works company in Vermont that did headstones for veterans.

"Chuck and Larry made it happen. Within a few weeks, we had a headstone for Andy's grave."

A memorial service was held in late April of 2012. The headstone was installed over Andy's grave.

"We had seven guys from A Battery who showed up for the service," Mel Major said. "Larry Kleinschmidt came. Jon Ringer and Carl Miller were there. There were around a dozen of Andy's relatives who came. It was like a healing for us, a closure, for everyone who attended."

ROY OSBORNE

"I enlisted and volunteered for Vietnam," Tennessee native Roy Osborne told me via a *Facebook* message. "I guess the best answer that I can give you is that I bought into the Domino Theory and I felt that 'it was my turn.' Make sense? I was 18 and fresh out of high school. I was a farm boy from a small community in middle Tennessee. There were 37 students in my high school graduating class and at the time, that was the largest class to graduate. My dad and his brothers had fought in WWII and Korea. My grandfathers were WWI veterans. My friends' families were the same for the most part. The growing anti-war sentiment had not reached our area yet. It was 1968 and the war was escalating. I didn't know where Vietnam was, but I had heard on the TV news that we must fight the terrible communists there, so we would not have to fight them in the United States. America was under threat ... and it was my turn.

"Boy, was I in for an eye-opening experience. Even after 18 months in Vietnam, getting more confused as to why we were there as each month went by, I came home proud of my service and still no idea that we would lose the war. (The United States of America did not lose wars.) I came home with a few ribbons on my chest and, I guess, wanting to hear the words 'thank you.' No one said that or even wanted to acknowledge that I had been away to war. It seemed the older veterans did not think we were fighting a real war and no one else had any interest in what was going on outside their own little world.

"I spent a couple of miserable years trying to hold down various jobs and just wanting to fit in. Finally, I went back on active duty and flourished until the Carter administration when the Army literally had a meltdown. I got out in 1978 as a Staff Sergeant E-6 with 27 months as a Drill Sergeant. I still didn't seem to fit in. I bought a semi-truck and spent the next 20 years on the road, until health problems forced me to retire.

"Yes, I am proud of my service, and yes, I would probably do it all over again."

ROBERT MILLER

"I was commissioned a second lieutenant from ROTC in May of 1964," Miller recalled. "Times and attitudes were much different then. We felt it was our duty. We had the best soldiers ... draftees, volunteers, NCOs and officers ... ever assembled. Too bad the government didn't tell these great soldiers what the war was all about, nor would they let us win it. That said, I would make the same choice."

CHAPTER FIFTEEN:
WHEN WILL WE EVER LEARN?

BABY BOOMERS DIDN'T INVENT THE protest movement. But we were the first generation whose dissatisfaction with government became a daily story on television. And that made all the difference. LBJ grudgingly told the nation in late March of 1968 that he would not seek his party's nomination for President later that year. He yielded his presidency because the impact of protests against an unpopular war in Vietnam tore the country apart. Richard M. Nixon succeeded LBJ and lost his presidency to a scandal first exposed by the *Washington Post* newspaper and then beaten to death on television every night. So maybe it was the ever-growing media, led by television, which really changed our world during the 1960s and 1970s.

My generation faced its litmus test when LBJ expanded the war in Vietnam, stepping up the draft to fulfill ever-increasing troop commitments. Those of us who ended up in the military tried to make the best of a bad situation. Besides possible death or dismemberment, serving in Vietnam exposed some of our soldiers to marijuana, hashish, opium and even heroin. It was part of the strategy of our enemy to make these drugs available to American soldiers. And as the war progressed, the drug problem among our soldiers out in the jungle got out of hand. Discipline broke down. Why should soldiers fight when anti-war protestors were winning their battle for the moral high ground back home in the early 1970s?

Many soldiers brought their drug problems home with them. Others, like myself, turned to alcohol and pot after we got home, for reasons open to individual interpretation. I don't blame the war for any problems I encountered during my transition into the real world. It was just me. Whatever mistakes I made, whatever regrets I have, are mine to own.

Very little attention was paid to all the Vietnam veterans who returned to their beloved country, went back to college or work, and began to push ahead with their lives. We didn't have many public role models to emulate. Soldier-turned-activist John Kerry was one, at least for those of us who believed the war was a bad idea. Mostly, though, Vietnam veterans infiltrated back into society, buried their past, and looked to the future. We were no different than veterans of any war. That's all we wanted, to be grouped with the men who had helped keep our country free over the past 200 years.

I do admit to carrying guilt over my stance against the Vietnam War. Some solace was gained when I read the words that retired Lt. General Hal Moore spoke at West Point in 2005. Moore was featured in Joe Galloway's iconic book about the Vietnam War: *"We Were Soldiers Once … and Young."* He had been commanding officer of an infantry unit that fought one of the first major battles of the war.

"In a long question-and-answer session following my (West Point) speech, I was asked about Iraq and then Defense Secretary Rumsfeld," Moore recalled in Galloway's fine sequel, *"We Are Soldiers Still."*

"In this place where cadets live by a code that says they never lie, cheat, steal or quibble – I was bound to speak the truth as I knew it. The war in Iraq, I said, is not worth the life of even one American soldier. As for Secretary Rumsfeld, I told them, I never thought I would live long enough to see someone chosen to preside over the Pentagon who made Vietnam-Era Defense Secretary Robert McNamara look good by comparison. The cadets sat in stunned silence; their professors were astonished. Some of these cadets would be leading young soldiers in combat in a matter of a few months. They deserved a straight answer."

McNamara, JFK's choice for Secretary of Defense, upped the ante in Vietnam, raising troop levels from 900 advisers in 1961 to 535,000 troops on the ground by 1968. He believed fully in his own statistical analysis of the war's outcome until doubts crept into his mind in 1967. He first offered to resign in November of 1967. LBJ allowed him to walk away on Feb. 29, 1968, right after the Tet Offensive ended in what our government called a "military stalemate." LBJ would offer his own resignation a month later when he chose not to run for President, or accept his party's nomination, in 1968.

McNamara finally publicly confessed in 1995 that the Vietnam War had been "wrong, terribly wrong." It was reported that MacNamara's close friend, Jacqueline Kennedy Onassis, helped change his opinion on the war over the years.

Another legendary general, Matt Ridgway, discouraged President Eisenhower from intervening in Vietnam after the French fell at Dien Bien Phu in 1954. At this point, Ridgway had risen to Chief of Staff of the Army. He prepared a detailed outline of what the United States military would have to do to achieve success in a jungle war not dissimilar from what our military had faced while fighting the Japanese 10 years earlier.

Ridgway correctly predicted, 10 years ahead of our full-scale commitment to Vietnam under LBJ, that our air power would not reduce the need for powerful and mobile ground forces to fight the VC and NVA in such a jungle-infested country. (McNamara must not have heard him.)

In the mid-1960s, LBJ asked the now-retired Ridgway for advice on Vietnam and the general told him it would be a mistake to get deeply involved in Indochina. In an article that appeared in *Foreign Affairs* magazine, Ridgway wrote that "political goals should be based on vital national interests and that military goals should be consistent with and support the political goals, but that neither situation was true in Vietnam." Again, how could our politicians and military leaders ignore such a warning from one of our great generals?

It is one thing for citizens to protest a war. It is quite another for reasonable generals to see Vietnam as a war we could not win. Ridgway saw this coming after serving in Korea. Moore made up his mind about Vietnam after two decades of contemplation and research.

It's the politicians who send our soldiers to war, often over economic issues that are camouflaged by loftier goals, like stopping the spread of communism, or bringing democracy to an oppressed society.

Moore's solution to the problem? Voters should select a commander-in-chief who won't rush into unnecessary wars.

"If we can't get that part right, then there will never be an end to the insanity that is war," Moore said in Galloway's sequel.

LBJ ignored the advice of Matthew Ridgway, and an elderly Douglas MacArthur, to pursue his goals in Vietnam. He listened instead to Robert McNamara, who had been a numbers-crunching Captain during World War II, devising flight schedules for military planes in the Pacific Theatre.

In the first Iraq War, President George H.W. Bush, himself a combat veteran of WWII, stopped the carnage after liberating Kuwait from Saddam Hussein. Bush understood that occupying Iraq would create serious problems for our soldiers. His son, however, wasn't as prudent, firing up the Iraq War again in 2003 and then occupying the country after driving Hussein from power. A war expected to last three months dragged on for 10 years, costing 4,500 soldiers their lives and countless more their chance for a normal life.

George W. Bush, who served in the Air National Guard during the Vietnam War, marched in tandem with his Vice President, Dick Cheney, recipient of five draft deferments during the 1960s.

Cheney toured the USA in 2013, promoting his new book and defending the Iraq War, rationalizing his failed predictions of a quick victory and a new government that would install democracy in that hub of the Middle East. One wonders, how many lives might have been saved if the young Dick Cheney found it in his busy schedule to submit to the draft and fight in Vietnam, slowing down or perhaps ending his political career before it began? How many soldiers who died in Vietnam might have gone on to live happy lives if LBJ hadn't listened to Bob McNamara? How many of our Iraq veterans might be living normal lives if the younger Bush hadn't rushed into an unnecessary war?

Vietnam veterans have learned to hold our heads high when discussing the controversial and unpopular war we fought in. We did answer the call to duty, pledging our faith to a country that was imploding during the 1960s. Anti-war protestors and conscientious objectors made their own hard decisions, either to avoid the draft or leave the country. They stood up for what they believed in, which is what our country is all about. Freedom. The right to make your own decisions.

Baby Boomers were forced to choose between country and conscience, only two decades after our parents' generation answered their clarion call in resounding fashion. That was the burden we faced. There was no evil Hitler for us, just a bearded little communist named Ho Chi Minh whom we knew nothing about.

Some of us were sucked up into the war machine, drafted out of real life, perhaps even eager to face the challenge that lay ahead. Others, like myself, went grudgingly, not wanting to make any waves. And then we went on with our lives.

I finally caught up with my old high school friend Jim Mazenko in the summer of 2012 at a cookout in John Coutts's backyard.

Jim told me what happened to him in the Army.

"I got drafted in October of 1966," he recalled, "and took advanced training at Fort Hood, Texas, specializing in the tank corps. I was a gunner. We were heading to Vietnam, no doubt about it. But two of my brothers were already serving in Southeast Asia, one in Vietnam and another in Laos. My congressman intervened and I was pulled from my unit before we got our orders for Vietnam. My sergeant was really pissed at me when I told him I wasn't going with them to Vietnam. He cussed me out, called me every name in the book. I found out later that the guys I trained with on my tank hit a mine in Vietnam and were killed. That was a terrible thing. You look back and think of how things could have been different in your life. I was lucky."

John Coutts, who had joined the Army Reserves back in the 1960s, is now connected to the Army through his daughter, Major Jaclyn (Coutts) Greiser, a lawyer who earned the 2013 Library of Congress' Burton Award for Public Service as a Special Victims Prosecutor.

"As a lawyer, Jaclyn found she could help people more in the Army than in private practice," John Coutts said. "We're very proud of her."

Another old high school pal, Tom DiIorio, attended the cookout with his son Mike, who completed a distinguished military career in the Navy. I had a chance to talk to Mike and was struck by the pride he took in his service. Two generations removed from Vietnam, the stain of a politicized war in Southeast Asia is only a faint memory for today's soldiers. And that's a good thing.

Those of us who served our country during the Vietnam War have a unique point of view. We participated in the most controversial war this country has ever fought (with the possible exception of Iraq II). We met soldiers from all over the country, learned from them, became friends with them, stood beside them during combat, and shared a complex bond of pride and brotherhood that will be broken only by death. My 2/32 artillery brothers are proud of the way our unit performed, not only during our time in Vietnam, but afterwards. The 2/32 performed with distinction between 1965-72 in Vietnam and even for a short time in Cambodia in 1970.

Looking back nearly 50 years into my past, I now understand that young and nervous teenager who went to war. He was just a kid with a lot to learn about the world. Socially and politically naïve, sure, and maybe a little curious about what lurked behind the next door. Too proud to hide, too well-trained by his parents to run. A perfect tool for our government to send to war.

ACKNOWLEDGEMENTS

THIS BOOK IS DEDICATED TO my brother Larry, who died in late February of 2012. Larry's passion for reading, especially American military history, inspired me to complete this book, which is based on true events.

Long-ago conversations have been recreated from memory, often with corrected details added by the people involved during the writing of this book. Several of my soldier friends provided their memories of events through email or over the phone.

One of the things I learned at our five FDC reunions is that everyone seemed to have a slightly different recollection of the same story. This book represents my version of the truth.

My brothers Dan and Tim looked over chapters related to family life. Several 2/32 veterans checked out the military chapters for mistakes. Chapter 13's stories on local veterans were based on interviews with the participants or their relatives. These stories originally appeared in both the *Pawtucket Times* and *Woonsocket Call* during 2011 and are reprinted here with appropriate accreditation. *Horizon Publications, Inc.* is the parent company of those two newspapers.

All of the characters in the book are real except for the free-lance journalist Jim Bowden and the female protestor at Penn State. Bowden was introduced in Chapter Five so that I could make a point or two about how the Vietnam War was covered by the media. The anti-war protestor in Chapter Nine was a composite of several students I met who marched against the war in the spring of 1971.

I have changed the names of several soldiers and civilians whom I couldn't contact during the writing of this book.

Cheryl Britland and her father, Bill, were integral to this book-writing process. Bill, a World War II vet who died in 2003, taught me how to take pride in being a veteran. His annual reunions of old Army Air Corps buddies were a big part of his life. And as death took away his fellow soldiers one by one, Bill kept on going to those reunions, remaining strong until it was his turn to move on. Cheryl shared my love of American history and prodded me to finish this book. She also added a strong final editing touch.

My old Army pals played a key role in the writing process, contributing their own oral histories and even reading certain chapters for accuracy's sake. I want to thank Larry Kleinschmidt in particular for reading the book with an editor's eye. Others who chipped in: Jon Ringer, Bill Kimball, Carl Miller, Tony Hoehner, Mel Major and the late Norm Gunderson.

Major Donald Babb also generously allowed me to publish excerpts of his memoirs, providing details about security changes at French Fort in August of 1968 that saved lives a month later when the enemy finally attacked our fire support base out in the middle of nowhere.

Thanks also go out to Chuck Healey, webmaster of the Proud Americans' website: **http://proudamericans.homestead.com**

This website's history of the 2/32 battalion, which was researched by Mel Major, provided exact dates of A Battery's movements during my tour. The website also serves as a meeting ground for many veterans. Most importantly, it made our first FDC reunion possible back in 2003, reuniting a group of soldiers who never thought they would see each other again.

OLD FRIENDS – These nine veterans of A Battery, 2/32 Artillery, held their fifth reunion in April, 2013. Pictured, front row, left to right: Bill Kimball, Mike Neisius, Chuck Rosenblum, Jon Ringer, Tom Barrett. Back row: Terry Nau, Bill Grelecki, Carl Miller, Tony Hoehner. (Photo by Carole Heffernan.)

Made in the USA
Charleston, SC
26 September 2013